A PINCH
OF SALT

**More
Everyday Expressions
from Scripture**

Timothy Cross

A PINCH
OF SALT

**More
Everyday Expressions
from Scripture**

Copyright © T. J. E. Cross, 2017
Paperback ISBN 978-1-5271-0027-5
Epub ISBN: 978-1-5271-0058-9
Mobi ISBN: 978-1-5271-0059-6

Published in 2017
by
Christian Focus Publications Ltd.
Geanies House, Fearn, Ross-shire,
IV20 1TW, Scotland, UK
www.christianfocus.com

Cover design by Daniel van Straaten

Printed by Bell and Bain, Glasgow

CONTENTS

Preface

The response to my previous book *A Little Bird Told Me: Everyday Expressions from Scripture* has been—and continues to be—most encouraging. Copies have been read all over the English-speaking world. A common remark has been along the lines of, 'You hear that expression all the time. I never knew that it came from the Bible.'

Unbeknown to many, expressions and sayings from the Bible have permeated our daily life in a profound way, and people are often amazed when it is pointed out that such sayings and expressions are actually biblical in origin. All this motivated me to research and write another compilation of 'Everyday Sayings from Scripture'—where the expressions and sayings originated, and how they apply to us today.

You now have the fruits of my labours in your hands! My prayer is that you will find it both interesting and enlightening, and, with the Lord's blessing, that it will give you a greater appreciation of the central message of the Bible, as encapsulated in its most famous verse: 'For God so loved the world that He gave His only begotten Son, that whoever believes in Him should not perish but have everlasting life' (John 3:16).

Timothy Cross
Cardiff, Wales

1

A friend in need is a friend indeed

'A friend in need is a friend indeed,' goes a saying. The expression means that it takes a time of trouble to reveal just who our true friends really are. There is such a phenomenon as a 'fair-weather friend'. These are our friends when all is well with us. But come a time of crisis—for example, unemployment, ill health, financial hardship, etc.—and a fair-weather friend is nowhere to be seen. A true friend though will stand by us during a time of trouble, and help and support us as best he or she can. Hence the saying: 'A friend in need is a friend indeed.'

The saying 'A friend in need is a friend indeed' is not found in the Bible verbatim, yet its sentiments are most definitely biblical, for in Proverbs 17:17 we read that 'A friend loves at all times, and a brother is born for adversity'—which means the same as our saying. Then in Proverbs 18:24 we read, 'A man *who has* friends must himself be friendly, but there is a friend *who* sticks closer than a brother.' If you have such a friend, you have good cause to get down on your knees and thank God for that person right now.

The problem is that our friends, being subject to human sinfulness and weakness, will always have the propensity to let us down—just as we are liable to let them down. The Lord Jesus, it is well known, chose twelve disciples 'that they might be with Him and that He might send them out to preach' (Mark 3:14). Of these twelve, one eventually betrayed Him, one disowned Him (denying he even knew Him), and, at the time of Jesus' greatest

9

need we read in Matthew 26:56 that 'all the disciples forsook Him and fled'.

While the Bible extols and celebrates human friendship—for example, Hannah and Ruth, Jonathan and David, Paul and Timothy, Peter and John—the emphasis of Scripture is on nothing less than divine friendship—knowing the friendship of and fellowship with Almighty God Himself. In grace, He actually enters into friendship with sinful human beings, and commits Himself to them for their earthly and eternal welfare. 'The secret of the LORD *is* with those who fear Him, and He will show them His covenant.' (Ps. 25:14). And when we consider again these verses from Proverbs—that 'A friend loves at all times, and a brother is born for adversity' and that 'there is a friend who sticks closer than a brother'—we may surely understand that these refer to the friendship of Jesus.

All Christians know and enjoy the friendship of Christ, and all Scripture ultimately points us to Him who is the living Word and who makes Himself present in the written Word. Of the Old Testament Scriptures, Jesus said that 'these are they which testify of Me' (John 5:39). And Scripture reveals that Jesus is a Friend indeed. We may let Him down, but He will never let us down.

Consider this in relation to both the cross of Christ and the companionship of Christ.

The Cross of Christ

Jesus said in John 15:13 that 'Greater love has no one than this, than to lay down one's life for his friends.' Then in 1 John 3:16 we read 'By this we know love, because He laid down His life for us.' Every believer can testify that the friendship of Jesus was so great that He actually gave His life for our salvation. He died an atoning death. He gave Himself as a sinless sacrifice to atone for our sins. He was punished to procure our pardon, and He endured the wrath of God to turn the wrath of God away from us. The cross of Christ was the supreme demonstration of the extent of the love of Jesus for His friends. He laid down His life for us so that we might have eternal life—that we might be reconciled to God and know fellowship with Him for evermore.

The Companionship of Christ

'And a brother is born for adversity,' says Proverbs. Our greatest need is for salvation. Jesus alone can meet us in our adversity here. And once we are saved, He continues to stand by us through all the ups and downs and losses and crosses of our earthly pilgrimage. The well-known hymn is absolutely right when it affirms 'What a Friend we have in Jesus.' He is truly 'a friend who sticks closer than a brother.' Good days and bad days, plenty and poverty, sickness and health, summer and winter, youth and old age ... the promises of Jesus have been well tested and well proved by His people throughout the ages: 'I will never fail you nor forsake you. Hence we can boldly say "*The LORD is my helper; I will not fear. What can man do to me?*"' (Heb. 13:6).

The apostle Paul's final letter was written from a Roman prison cell to my namesake, Timothy. Paul was facing imminent execution. Almost his final recorded words summarise what we have said in this chapter. They testify on the one hand to the unreliability of human friendship, but on the other hand to the total dependability of the Lord Jesus Christ. Paul wrote: 'At my first defense no one stood with me, but all forsook me. May it not be charged against them. But the Lord stood with me and strengthened me, so that the message might be preached fully through me, and *that* all the Gentiles might hear. Also I was delivered out of the mouth of the lion' (2 Tim. 4:16-17).

'But the Lord stood with me,' said Paul. 'A friend in need is a friend indeed.' Jesus is a friend indeed. He gave His life to save us. He continues to stand by us. He never fails us. He never forsakes us.

> One there is, above all others,
> Well deserves the name of Friend;
> His is love beyond a brother's,
> Costly, free, and knows no end:
> They who once His kindness prove,
> Find it everlasting love!
>
> Which of all our friends to save us,
> Could or would have shed their blood?
> But our Jesus died to have us
> Reconciled, in Him to God:
> This was boundless love indeed!
> Jesus is a Friend in need.
>
> When He lived on earth abased,
> Friend of sinners was His name;
> Now, above all glory raised;
> He rejoices in the same,
> Still He calls them brethren, friends:
> And to all their wants attends.
>
> O for grace our hearts to soften!
> Teach us, Lord, at length to love,
> We alas! forget too often;
> What a Friend we have above,
> But when home our souls are brought:
> We will love Thee as we ought.
>
> (John Newton, 1725–1807)

2

A heavy heart

In Proverbs 25:20 we read, 'He who sings songs to a heavy heart is like one who takes off a garment on a cold day, and like vinegar on a wound' (RSV). '*Like* one who takes away a garment in cold weather, *and like* vinegar on soda, *is* one who sings songs to a heavy heart.' The verse is a reminder to us that we should always be sensitive to others, for we might not know what inner burdens they are carrying. If we should behave in a wrong or inappropriate way towards them, we might make a bad situation worse. How we need to seek wisdom from the Lord, and ask Him to give us sensitivity and tact in our dealings with others.

It is from this verse, Proverbs 25:20, that we get the well-known expression 'a heavy heart'. Proverbs 12:25a is similar when it says, 'Anxiety in a man's heart weighs him down' (RSV). A 'heavy heart' cannot be measured on bathroom scales, yet if we are suffering with this condition, we know that it weighs us down in a manner no less real than if someone had placed an overloaded rucksack on our back. By using the term 'heart', we are referring to our inner being, and the experience of having something overwhelming on our minds, giving us tunnel vision, prohibiting us from thinking of much else but the matter which weighs us down.

The Causes of a Heavy Heart
The causes of a heavy heart are manifold. At college we face the pressure of exams, the passing of which determines our future. Next we may know the anxiety of being unemployed—or in a job which we do not feel is quite suitable for us. Debt

and money worries are responsible for many a heavy heart. Then there are the anxieties about our loved ones—maybe our children's physical and spiritual wellbeing, or perhaps our elderly parents' declining mental and physical powers. Many and varied circumstances, and our own sense of inadequacy to deal with them, can so easily degenerate into an overriding anxiety that is with us day and night. 'Anxiety in a man's heart weighs him down ...' If you are a stranger to the experience of 'a heavy heart', I suggest you should get down on your knees right now and thank God. He has been exceedingly merciful to you. Most of us are not so blessed.

The Remedy for a Heavy Heart

We are told that a healthy, physical heart may be maintained by the right diet and regular exercise. But what is the remedy for a 'heavy heart'—the more subtle, but exceedingly real, mental and spiritual malady we experience when something weighs so heavily on our mind? The Bible gives the answer—a remedy which is both simple and effective and has been well proved throughout the ages. Psalm 55:22 guides us in these words: 'Cast your burden on the LORD, and He shall sustain you.' Peter takes up this verse in 1 Peter 5:7 when he writes that we are to be 'casting all your care upon Him, for He cares for you [us].'

As Christians, we have a God to Whom we may turn when the burdens of this life weigh us down. We have a loving, heavenly Father. We have a sympathetic Saviour who knows all too well our human condition and what it is like to suffer. We are promised the help and strength of God's Holy Spirit—known throughout the ages as the divine comforter, the 'Parakletos'—the One called alongside to help. So the good news is that we do not have to bear our burdens alone. The God of the Bible—the God revealed

14

supremely in the Lord Jesus Christ—has promised to relieve us of our burdens. To understate it: He who sustains this vast universe is infinitely capable of bearing our burdens! If He does not see fit to take them from us, He will most surely strengthen us to bear them, for He has promised in these wonderful words that '[His] grace is sufficient for you' (2 Cor. 12:9).

So, all Christians have the privilege of unburdening their burdens on Almighty God Himself. As the hymn writer expressed it, 'Are we weak and heavy laden, cumbered with a load of care? We should never be discouraged, take it to the Lord in prayer.'[1]

Jesus, our Saviour, bore our greatest burden at Calvary, for there He bore our sins and God's judgement on them. '[He] Himself bore our sins in His own body on the tree' (1 Pet. 2:24). And Jesus still gives us the wonderful invitation to cast our burdens on Him, whatever they may be. Some of His most famous words were in the form of an invitation to those suffering from a heavy heart. They are found in Matthew 11:28: 'Come to Me, all *you* who labor and are heavy laden, and I will give you rest.' Jesus is the great Burden Bearer. He is the great reliever of all who come to Him suffering from a heavy heart.

> Beautiful words of Jesus,
> Spoken so long ago,
> Yet, as we sing them over,
> Dearer to us they grow,
> Calling the heavy laden,
> Calling to hearts oppressed,
> Come unto Me, ye weary;
> Come, I will give you rest.

---

1. Quoted from the hymn by Joseph Scriven, 'What a Friend We Have in Jesus'.

A Pinch of Salt

Beautiful words of Jesus,
Cheering us, day by day;
Throwing a gleam of sunshine
Over a cloudy way;
Casting on Him the burden
We are too weak to bear,
He will give grace sufficient,
He will regard our prayer.

o---0---o

Hear the call of His voice, so sweet;
Bring your load to the Savior's feet;
Lean your heart on His loving breast,
Come, O come, He will give you rest.

(Eliza E. Hewitt, 1851–1920)

3
A house divided

A recent slump in form of the English cricket team was blamed on 'a divided dressing room'. A certain player had made comments about his teammates on social media, and this caused alienation and disharmony among the team until all was sorted out. The team and selectors were described in the news bulletins as 'a house divided', and this division was seen to be the cause of the English cricket team's departure from winning ways. The saying proved true. It was a case of 'united we stand, divided we fall'.

It is perhaps not very well known that the expression concerning 'a house divided' originates from the lips of the Lord Jesus Christ. In the earthly ministry of Jesus, we see that something of the age to come—the kingdom of heaven—invaded the present age. We thus see Jesus performing many miracles of physical and spiritual healing, and casting out demons from those oppressed by the devil. Jesus transformed the lives of many, bringing new life, new hope and new joy. Yet, very surprisingly, Jesus had His enemies. Instead of rejoicing in the miracles which authenticated Christ's ministry, the Pharisees scornfully accused and opposed Him and said: 'This *fellow* does not cast out demons except by Beelzebub, the ruler of the demons' (Matt. 12:24). Blasphemously, therefore, there were those who attributed Christ's power not to God but to Satan. By way of response, Jesus made them think of the logical implication of their accusation. And in doing so, He gave us our expression. Jesus said:

'Every kingdom divided against itself is brought to desolation, and every city or house divided against itself

17

will not stand. And if Satan casts out Satan, he is divided against himself. How then will his kingdom stand? And if I cast out demons by Beelzebub, by whom do your sons cast *them* out? Therefore they shall be your judges. But if I cast out demons by the Spirit of God, surely the kingdom of God has come upon you '(Matt. 12:25–28).

Only the power of God explains the deeds which the Lord Jesus did. As Jesus said, 'The works which the Father has given Me to finish—the very works that I do—bear witness of Me, that the Father has sent Me' (John 5:36).

In 1 John 3:8 we read the succinct statement that 'For this purpose the Son of God was manifested, that He might destroy the works of the devil.' Back in Eden at the dawn of history, it was Satan who tempted our first ancestors to sin against God and disobey His revealed will. Sadly, Adam and Eve succumbed to this temptation, and, in doing so, brought misery on themselves and on all their descendants. They spoiled the fellowship with God their Maker they had previously enjoyed.

We have inherited their sinful nature, and thus, apart from the saving grace of God, we, too, are alienated from our Maker. But Jesus came to put things right. In Eden, God promised that, in the fullness of time, one of Eve's descendents would come and undo the ravages which Satan had wrought, fatally bruising Satan's head, while Himself being bruised in the process. In the Lord Jesus and in His atoning death on the cross, the promise was most wonderfully fulfilled. The reason the Son of God appeared was to destroy the works of the devil. He 'disarmed principalities and powers [and], He made a public spectacle of them, triumphing over them in it [the cross]' (Col. 2:15).

Jesus therefore came on a mission to undo the ravages which Satan had wrought. Satan is mighty, but Jesus is even mightier. Jesus went on to describe Himself as the One who enters Satan's 'house' (that is, this world, where Satan holds sway) and binds the strong man so that He can plunder his goods (Matt. 12:29). To attribute Jesus' power to Satan, therefore, as the Pharisees did, was as ludicrous as it was blasphemous—and by its very nature doing so is the only unpardonable sin. If Satan was indeed 'casting out Satan', his house was divided and would surely fall. Satan would not cast out Satan as he is more than keen to hold on to his subjects. Jesus, however, did come to cast out Satan. He bound him and plundered his goods. As Peter explained to Cornelius and his household some years later: 'God anointed Jesus of Nazareth with the Holy Spirit and with power, who went about doing good and healing all who were oppressed by the devil, for God was with Him' (Acts 10:38).

Paradoxically, it was when Jesus was on the cross, when Satan seemed victorious, that he received his fatal blow. Satan caused a rupture between us and our Maker, but in dying on the cross for our sins, Jesus reconciles to God all who believe in Him. It is the cross of Christ—the Christ of the cross—who ultimately destroys the devil's work. 'Christ also suffered once for sins, the just for the unjust, that He might bring us to God' (1 Pet. 3:18). While Satan was the alienating destroyer, Jesus is the reconciling Deliverer. Every Christian can testify that this is so, for 'when we were enemies we were reconciled to God through the death of His Son' (Rom. 5:10). 'We … rejoice in God through our Lord Jesus Christ, through whom we have now received the reconciliation' (Rom. 5:11).

'No house divided against itself will stand,' said the Lord Jesus when the Pharisees accused Him of doing the devil's work. The Pharisees see Jesus as the devil's agent, despite the transparent goodness of His work. If they were right, Satan would be set on a suicide course—as are all who, like the Pharisees, call good evil. They are stubbornly denying the Holy Spirit's work, and making their own forgiveness impossible.[1]

---

1. *The Lion Handbook to the Bible*, p. 483, David and Pat Alexander, Lion Publishing, Berkhamsted, 1973.

4

A pinch of salt

'You must take this with a pinch of salt.' You hear this expression when people don't want you completely to believe what they are saying. Perhaps they are exaggerating. Or perhaps they are expressing a wish or aspiration, rather than describing reality. 'Take it with a pinch of salt.' The expression is not found in the Bible, because the Bible uniformly commands us always to speak the truth. 'Therefore, putting away lying, "*Let* each one   speak truth with his neighbor"...' (Eph. 4:25). Yet if we know our Bible, we can trace 'pinches of salt' in its pages—pinches of salt which are positive and life affirming, rather than negative or shady.

The Salt of the Covenant

In Numbers 18:19 and 2 Chronicles 13:5 we read of the 'covenant of salt' which the Lord God made with His people. The covenant is central to the Bible, for the Bible unfolds God's everlasting covenant of grace to save a people for Himself and for His glory. The covenant refers to God's gracious pledge and promise to be God to His people for time and eternity. The initiative in the covenant is always God's. It is sovereignly administered—yet He expects us to love and obey Him in response. The Bible is divided into the Old and New Covenants. There is, however, but one covenant of grace, and this was administered differently by God in the different eras of the Old and New Covenants. The covenant reached its climax and culmination in the Lord Jesus Christ. In Matthew 26:28, we read His words: 'For this is My blood of the new covenant, which is shed for many for the remission of sins.' It is by the atoning death of Jesus that we enter into fellowship with God for time and eternity, and so experience the blessing of God's covenant. And if God is truly our God, and has bound Himself to us in grace, all can only be well. He will undertake for us for time and eternity. But what has this got to do with 'a pinch of salt'? The New Bible Dictionary explains, stating that salt

> was often used among Oriental peoples for ratifying agreements, so that salt became the symbol of fidelity and constancy. In the Levitical cereal offerings (Leviticus 2:13) salt was used as a preservative to typify the eternal nature of the 'covenant of salt' existing between God and Israel.[1]

The Salt of the Christian

Before the days of the deep freeze, salt was used as a preservative for food. Like today, it also gave food added flavour. In His well-known Sermon on the Mount the Lord Jesus, in Matthew 5:13, says to His followers, 'You are the salt of the earth; but if the salt loses its flavor, how shall it be seasoned? It is then good for nothing but to be thrown out and trampled underfoot by men.'

We have just seen that salt symbolises God's faithfulness and commitment to His people. So here, the Lord Jesus is first of all exhorting us to be the people we are—to live as the covenant people of God; to live in gratitude and obedience to Him; to live as the beneficiaries of His grace and favour; to live for the praise of His glory.

Yet surely, secondly, Jesus also had the preserving and flavouring uses of salt in mind when He spoke the above words. No one would deny that our twenty-first century society is rotten—it is characterised by moral decay and blatantly flouts the commandments of God. Christians, nevertheless, are called

---

1. J.D. Douglas, Editor, *New Bible Dictionary* (Second Edition), Leicester, IVP, 1982, Salt, p. 1056.

to be different. We are called to be holy and wholesome, and even to do what we can to stem the moral decay. And aren't we also called to be flavoursome—to make the Christian life seem desirable and attractive? The Christian life truly is an incomparable life. If we belong to Jesus, our sins are forgiven, we have been adopted into the family of God and we are heirs of eternal life. We have just reason to be the happiest people on the planet. Oh though that this would be manifest to those around us! Jesus would have it so. 'You are the salt of the earth,' He says. You are to live to the praise of God, to swim against the immoral tide and make the Christian faith desirable and attractive.

The Salt of Conversation
In Colossians 4:6, Paul's exhortation to all Christians is to '*Let* your speech always *be* with grace, seasoned with salt, that you may know how you ought to answer each one.' A Christian, therefore, is to be characterised by wholesome, godly speech. Blasphemy and foul language may be heard all around us, but this is incompatible from one born again of the Spirit of God. The gospel transforms every area of our being—how we think, how we act and how we speak. Our tongue reveals the state of our heart—what we are like inside. Jesus said in Luke 6:45 that 'A good man out of the good treasure of his heart brings forth good; and an evil man out of the evil treasure of his heart brings forth evil. For out of the abundance of the heart his mouth speaks.' So seek God's grace to be a Christian in conversation as well as conduct. '*Let* your speech always *be* with grace, seasoned with salt ...'

So, 'a pinch of salt' is not an exact biblical expression—yet the Bible does have its pinches of salt for us to consider. Thank God for His covenant of grace. His love will not let us go. In response, seek to be a salty Christian in word and deed—faithful to God, and as wholesome and pure as it is possible for a saved sinner to be.

5

A prophet is not without honour

Slight variations on the above saying are sometimes heard. For example: 'A prophet is not without honour except in his own country.' The saying is quoted when people fail to recognise the greatness of one of their own, and perhaps treat such a person less than well. This can sometimes be a case of familiarity breeding contempt, or even a manifestation of a jealous spirit.

Here is an international opera singer. He receives great applause wherever he performs throughout the world. But his neighbours at home are not interested in opera. They just pass the time of day with him when they see him in the supermarket or mowing his lawn.

Or take the case of Muhammad Ali, the boxer. As the young Cassius Clay, he won an Olympic gold medal. But when he returned home to Louisville, instead of being acclaimed as 'a local boy made good', on entering a café he was told, 'We don't serve negroes here.' His reply was quick witted: 'That's OK, as I don't eat them.' Such instances of mistreatment are a case of 'A prophet is not without honour except in his own country.'

The saying concerning 'a prophet is not without honour ...' was uttered by none less than the Lord Jesus Christ when He returned to His earthly home in Nazareth one day. It is a matter of debate as to whether the Saviour originated the saying, or whether He was using a saying that was well known for His own purposes. In John 4:44 we simply read these words: 'For Jesus Himself testified that a prophet has no honor in his own country.'

The incident which triggered off this saying is related to us in Mark 6:1-6 where it is written:

> Then He went out from there and came to His own country, and His disciples followed Him. And when the Sabbath had come, He began to teach in the synagogue. And many hearing *Him* were astonished, saying, 'Where *did* this *Man get* these things? And what wisdom is this which is given to Him, that such mighty works are performed by His hands! Is this not the carpenter, the Son of Mary, and brother of James, Joses, Judas, and Simon? And are not His sisters here with us?' And they were offended at Him.
>
> But Jesus said to them, 'A prophet is not without honor except in his own country, among his own relatives, and in his own house.' Now He could do no mighty work there, except that He laid His hands on a few sick people and healed *them*. And He marveled because of their unbelief.

So the people of Nazareth—the place where Jesus was nurtured as a boy, and where He initially worked as a carpenter as a young man—failed to recognise His true identity and to give Him the honour which He is due as the Son of God and as God the Son. They well remembered Him plying His carpenter's trade, but, as far as they were concerned, He was no more than the village carpenter. He was just an ordinary Nazarene, and nothing else. They thus rejected their most famous Son. 'He came to His own, and His own did not receive Him' (John 1:11). John 7:5 records that 'even His brothers did not believe in Him'. So the Lord Jesus knew from painful, personal experience that 'A prophet is not without honor except in his own country, among his own relatives, and in his own house'. The mistake which those Nazarenes made here could not have been more fatal, for Scripture says,

'Whoever denies the Son does not have the Father either; he who acknowledges the Son has the Father also' (1 John 2:23).

The question is: Why did the people of Nazareth fail to recognise the true identity of Jesus and honour Him accordingly? And why do not all people in the world recognise Jesus and honour Him as the Son of God and cast themselves on Him for the salvation so desperately needed? According to the Bible, we will only truly recognise Jesus if God Himself, by His Spirit, reveals His true identity to us. The evidence for Christ's deity is all there in the Bible, yet by nature we are blind to it. It is spiritually discerned. Jesus once asked His disciples, 'Who do you say that I am?' (Matt. 16:15). 'Simon Peter answered and said, "You are the Christ, the Son of the living God"' (Matt. 16:16). Pertinently, Matthew then relates that 'Jesus answered and said to him, "Blessed are you, Simon Bar-Jonah, for flesh and blood has not revealed this to you, but My Father who is in heaven"' (Matt. 16:17).

So we conclude by stating that it takes a miracle of divine grace to truly recognise Jesus and embrace the good news of salvation which He alone brings to sinners. By nature we are blind to His glories. 'The god of this age has blinded [the minds of those], who do not believe, lest the light of the gospel of the glory of Christ, who is the image of God, should shine on them' (2 Cor. 4:4). Christians, however, have a testimony to relate. They view Jesus in an infinitely different way from those Nazarenes who considered that He was no more than the local carpenter— and infinitely differently from those who consider Him as merely a teacher, preacher and moral example from the first-century Middle East. He is the Son of God and God the Son! He is the Second Person of the Trinity. He is the only Saviour of sinners. He is our Saviour.

How is this difference in attitude towards the Lord Jesus explained? Only by the distinguishing working of God Himself. 'For it is the God who commanded light to shine out of darkness who has shone in our hearts to *give* the light of the knowledge of the glory of God in the face of Jesus Christ' (2 Cor. 4:6).

Sadly and tragically, the people of Nazareth failed to recognise the identity of one of their own. Jesus was a prophet without honour in His own country. Even though 'He came to His own, and His own did not receive Him' (John 1:11), praise God that the following verses are as equally true. 'But as many as received Him, to them He gave the right to become children of God, to those who believe in His name: who were born, not of blood, nor of the will of the flesh, nor of the will of man, but of God' (John 1:12-13).

6

A word in season

'[A] word *spoken* in due season, how good *it is!*' states Proverbs 15:23. The book of Proverbs goes back to King Solomon's day, some 1500 years B.C.—yet the saying 'a word in season' is still in everyday use. 'A word in season' refers to something which someone says to us which lifts us up and encourages us, just when we needed lifting up and encouraging. 'A word in season' is thus a welcome word, coming just at the right time—a word which lifts a burden and puts iron into our souls. Elsewhere, the book of Proverbs states what we all know from personal experience: 'Anxiety in the heart of man causes depression, but a good word makes it glad' (Prov. 12:25).

The Gospel: A Word Always in Season
Proverbs 25:25 says, '*As* cold water to a weary soul, so *is* good news from a far country.' The gospel of Christ is truly 'good news from a far country' as it is good news from heaven itself. The original gospel message was actually beamed from heaven to earth. It was spoken not by a man, but by an angel who proclaimed the welcome news to some frightened shepherds in the fields surrounding Bethlehem: 'Do not be afraid, for behold, I bring you good tidings of great joy which will be to all people. For there is born to you this day in the city of David a Savior, who is Christ the Lord' (Luke 2:10-11).

The gospel of Christ is a message of divine mercy to lost, condemned sinners. It truly is 'a word in season' and will be received and welcomed as such until Christ comes again in glory, and God's eternal purpose of grace is complete. The Holy Spirit of

God has a convicting role. It is He who convinces us that we are in a perilous state—sinners in the hands of an angry God, liable to be declared 'guilty' before the divine tribunal, and thus to be sentenced—cast into the flames of eternal hell for who we are and what we have done. The same Holy Spirit, however, also makes Jesus real to us. He makes the gospel known to us—that 'Christ Jesus came into the world to save sinners' (1 Tim. 1:15). This message of mercy is 'a word in season' like no other. It truly is music to the sinner's ears. It proclaims that Christ died to procure our forgiveness, deliver us from the wrath of God and ensure that we will be declared eternally righteous in God's sight. The Holy Spirit enables us to receive this glad message, embrace Christ as our Saviour and so appropriate all the blessings and benefits of divine salvation.

The gospel of Christ, it is 'a word in season' truly known by Christians alone:

> Redemption! Oh, wonderful story–
> Glad message for you and for me;
> That Jesus has purchased our pardon,
> And paid all the debt on the tree.

(Samuel M. Sayford, born 1846)

Giving a Word in Season

We must never underestimate the power of our words for either good or ill, either for edification or for destruction. Words can wound and words can help. 'There is one who speaks like the piercings of a sword, but the tongue of the wise *promotes* health' (Prov. 12:18).

It was written prophetically of the Lord Jesus that, 'The Lord God has given Me the tongue of the learned, that I should know how to speak a word in season to *him who is* weary' (Isa. 50:4). When the Lord Jesus spoke, therefore, He always spoke 'a word in season'. If we belong to Him, we are surely called to do the same. It is sobering to read in the Bible that the Lord Jesus warned, 'I say to you that for every idle word men may speak, they will give account of it in the day of judgment' (Matt. 12:36).

The words which we habitually speak are a barometer of our heart. A careless word can be akin to throwing away a match carelessly. It can ignite a fire and cause havoc, destruction and misery. Christians are thus called to be Christians in thought, word and deed—by what we say and what we do not say, as well as by what we do and think. Hence Paul's exhortation to 'Let no corrupt word proceed out of your mouth, but what is good for necessary edification, that it may impart grace to the hearers' (Eph. 4:29).

So we return to our expression, and can only concur that 'a word *spoken* in due season, how good *it is!*' (Prov. 15:23). Thank God for the Word of salvation—the gospel of Christ. Thank God for those He has sent to us to deliver 'a word in season' just when we needed it. And by His grace, let us also seek to be channels of 'a word in season' to those around us who are in need.

A careless word may kindle strife
A cruel word may wreck a life
A bitter word may hate instil
A brutal word may smite and kill
A gracious word may smooth the way
A joyous word may light the day
A timely word may lessen stress
A loving word may heal and bless.[1]

---

1. 'The War Cry' quoted in *Pocket Wisdom,* compiled by Robert C. Savage, p. 133, Tyndale House Publishers, Wheaton, 1984.

7

An eye for an eye

'I was just getting my retaliation in first,' said a politician a while ago. I for one found the expression amusing. There is also a saying—a saying which is completely unbiblical—which goes 'Don't get mad; get even.' A saying which people quote with a vague idea that it comes from the Bible, however, is 'An eye for an eye and a tooth for a tooth.' Popularly, this refers to 'getting your own back' when someone has treated you badly.

Old Testament Law

The expression 'an eye for an eye' has its origin in the Old Testament, in the law of Moses. In Leviticus 24:19-20 it is written that 'If a man causes disfigurement of his neighbor, as he has done, so shall it be done to him—fracture for fracture, eye for eye, tooth for tooth; as he has caused disfigurement of a man, so shall it be done to him.'

To our ears, 'an eye for an eye' sounds rather brutal, harsh and uncivilised. The saying, however, is not actually as harsh as it sounds—especially when viewed against the background and context of the violent times in which it was originally given. The law of Moses is teaching here that justice must be strictly proportionate to the crime committed and not be 'over the top'.

Here is a dispute between two men. They fight. One knocks the other's tooth out. Before the days of advanced dental treatment, this would mean being without that tooth for life. The other man then tries to 'knock his block off'. The Old Testament law, however, prohibited meting out such justice. Justice had to be strictly proportionate—'fracture for fracture, eye for eye, tooth for

33

tooth ...' Exodus 21:23-25 states the principle similarly: 'You shall give life for life, eye for eye, tooth for tooth, hand for hand, foot for foot, burn for burn, wound for wound, stripe for stripe.' So the law of Moses does teach 'an eye for an eye'—but no more than an eye. Justice was not to be disproportionate to the crime.

New Testament Grace

When we turn to the New Testament, however, we see that the Old Testament saying 'an eye for an eye' has been superseded—it has been revised in the light of God's fuller revelation of Himself in Christ. The Lord Jesus, in His well-known Sermon on the Mount, said:

> 'You have heard that it was said, "An eye for an eye and a tooth for a tooth." But I tell you not to resist an evil person. But whoever slaps you on your right cheek, turn the other to him also. If anyone wants to sue you and take away your tunic, let him have *your* cloak also. And whoever compels you to go one mile, go with him two. Give to him who asks you, and from him who wants to borrow from you do not turn away.
>
> 'You have heard that it was said, "You shall love your neighbor and hate your enemy." But I say to you, love your enemies, bless those who curse you, do good to those who hate you, and pray for those who spitefully use you and persecute you, that you may be sons of your Father in heaven; for He makes His sun rise on the evil and on the good, and sends rain on the just and on the unjust' (Matt. 5:38-45).

The Old Testament law taught a judicious, personal retaliation. The Lord Jesus, however, taught that we should not retaliate at all. He even enjoins on us love for our enemies—to desire and promote their good, even when they do us harm. Of course, this all reveals the necessity of being born again. How we need the transforming grace of God. Yet the commandment of the Lord Jesus is inexplicable apart from the gospel of God's saving grace in Christ.

The gospel proclaims that God Himself has not meted out strict justice upon us for our sins against Him. Rather, in His mercy, He sent His Son to die for us—to take our sins upon Himself and to bear God's wrath that was due us so that we might be delivered from it. 'In this is love, not that we loved God, but that He loved us and sent His Son *to be* the propitiation for our sins' (1 John 4:10).

As Christians, we are enjoined to be merciful to our enemies because God has been merciful to us. We were once God's enemies—sin is an affront to Him—but God has shown grace to us. 'For if when we were enemies we were reconciled to God through the death of His Son, much more, having been reconciled, we shall be saved by His life' (Rom. 5:10). If we belong to Jesus, we are the recipients of the mercy of God. How incongruous it is, then, for us not to show mercy to others! How incongruous it is, in the light of the gospel, for a Christian to hold a vendetta, and be out for his or her 'pound of flesh'—to seek 'an eye for an eye'! God has shown grace to sinners like you and me. Therefore we should show grace to our enemies.

'An eye for an eye.' The saying has no place in a Christian's life. But what of our enemies? Isn't the desire for vengeance when we have been hurt and harmed a natural one? Yes, it is. But Christians have been transformed by the grace of God. And why do we have to take action against our enemies in any case? Do we not have a God to whom we can turn? Is He not in absolute control of all things? Surely we can safely leave our enemies in His hands. He can deal with them far better than we can! The Scripture states: 'Beloved, do not avenge yourselves, but *rather* give place to wrath; 'for it is written, "Vengeance is Mine, I will repay," says the Lord' (Rom. 12:19).

Peter once wrote to some believers who were suffering at the hand of their persecutors. When he did, he focussed their attention on Calvary, the centre of the centre of the Christian faith. Jesus, too, suffered at the hands of His persecutors, Peter reminded them. So when Jesus was accomplishing our salvation, Peter wrote, He, 'when He was reviled, did not revile in return; when He suffered, He did not threaten, but committed *Himself* to Him who judges righteously' (1 Pet. 2:23). And so we leave the matter of the judgement of our enemies to God and we do not take the matter into our own, clumsy hands. Peter goes on to conclude: 'Therefore let those who suffer according to the will of God commit their souls *to Him* in doing good, as to a faithful Creator' (1 Pet. 4:19). Our enemies are unable to snatch us out of our Saviour's hands!

8

Another one bites the dust

The expression 'Another one bites the dust' is sometimes used in the sporting world. It refers to a time when either a team or an individual is on a victorious, winning streak, defeating all the opponents which are set against them. When someone 'bites the dust' the picture is one of their defeat and even humiliation.

Psalm 72 was originally a Psalm about King Solomon and his reign. The Psalm, however, transcends Solomon's kingship and, with its promise of universal peace and prosperity, points us to the Lord Jesus Christ and the final establishment of the kingdom which His second coming in glory will inaugurate. And so we read:

> In His days the righteous shall flourish,
> And abundance of peace,
> Until the moon is no more.
> He shall have dominion also from sea to sea,
> And from the River to the ends of the earth.
> Those who dwell in the wilderness will bow before Him,
> And His enemies will lick the dust.
> The kings of Tarshish and of the isles
> Will bring presents;
> The kings of Sheba and Seba
> Will offer gifts.
> Yes, all kings shall fall down before Him;
> All nations shall serve Him (Ps. 72:7-11)

'*His enemies will lick the dust.*' I italicised those words. Here we see the origin of the popular expression 'to bite the dust'. It goes back to King Solomon's day, around 1000 years B.C., but the saying truly applies to the Lord Jesus Christ, for He is the King of kings and Lord of lords. The Bible informs us that on a coming day, universal homage will be made to Him and 'that at the name of Jesus every knee should bow, of those in heaven, and of those on earth, and of those under the earth, and *that* every tongue should confess that Jesus Christ *is* Lord, to the glory of God the Father' (Phil. 2:10,11).

'May His foes bow down before Him, and may His enemies lick the dust,' we may well pray from Psalm 72. All of Christ's enemies will most surely 'lick the dust' one day, for there is none greater than the Lord Jesus Christ. His final words on earth were, 'All authority has been given to Me in heaven and on earth' (Matt. 28:18). All power and authority is Christ's, and He actually exercises and will yet exercise that power and authority. The Bible reveals that Christ conquers His enemies in two ways—that is in a present conquest and a pending conquest.

Christ's Present Conquest

Christ's universal kingship and authority is a facet of His being the Messiah, wherein He combines the roles of prophet, priest and king in His one Person. The *Westminster Shorter Catechism* states of Him in His kingship that 'Christ executeth the office of a king in subduing us to Himself, in ruling and defending us, and in restraining and conquering all His and our enemies.'[1]

Lawson's comment on this makes the point that:

> A king is a ruler of a kingdom. Now there is a great kingdom set up on earth, consisting of all God's people and its ruler is Christ. As such, His duties are here said to be threefold.

---

1. Answer to Question 26 in the *Westminster Shorter Catechism*.

1. He makes us willing to obey Him. 2. He gives us laws for our guidance and safety. 3. He limits and finally puts down all who oppose us and Him.[2]

Every Christian has gladly bowed down to Christ. He has conquered us by His love and grace. God, in Christ, has actually made His enemies His friends, for the Bible says 'when we were enemies we were reconciled to God through the death of His Son' (Rom. 5:10). It is our sin which makes us enemies of God and rebels against His kingdom. He is opposed to sin. It is an affront to His holy nature and disobedience against His authority. But in His mercy, God sent His Son to deal with our sin and so remove the cause of hostility between us—'that He might reconcile them both to God in one body through the cross, thereby putting to death the enmity' (Eph. 2:16).

Christ's Pending Conquest

Christians have gladly and willingly 'bowed the knee' to King Jesus. But the Bible reveals that on a coming day, everyone will bow before Him. 'For He must reign till He has put all enemies under His feet' (1 Cor. 15:25). When Jesus comes again in glory, truly His enemies will bow down before Him and lick the dust. He will bring in His eternal kingdom of righteousness and peace. He will destroy all who are opposed to Him and all that is incompatible and contrary to His reign. Those who belong to Him will know eternal bliss—but all those who have rebelled against Him—they 'shall have their part in the lake which burns with fire and brimstone, which is the second death' (Rev. 21:8).

---

2. *Shorter Catechism with commentary and Scripture Proofs*, Rev Roderick Lawson, The Sabbath School Society for Ireland (n.d.), p. 21.

Jesus shall reign! All the enemies of Christ will, one day, most surely bite the dust. God will fulfil His eternal purpose of grace and glory 'according to the purpose of Him who works all things according to the counsel of His will' (Eph. 1:11). He cannot be thwarted, frustrated or defeated. He will most surely right all wrongs. Paradise lost will become Paradise restored.

When we see the evils rampant in the world, and so much that is condoned that is contrary to the revealed will of God, we may find that we become impatient with the ways of the Almighty. Why does He not make all His enemies lick the dust right now? The Bible's answer is because God is patient, longsuffering and merciful.

Today is a day of grace. God's enemies still may believe in Christ and so be delivered from the judgement to come. Jesus has never yet and will never turn any repentant sinner away. Peter wrote the following words to those who were getting impatient over the seeming delay over Christ's second coming in glory: 'The Lord is not slack concerning *His* promise, as some count slackness, but is longsuffering toward us, not willing that any should perish but that all should come to repentance' (2 Pet. 3:9). I thank God that He gave me time to believe in Jesus before He came again. If you believe in Jesus, you have the same cause to thank Him, too. But Jesus will most surely come again. God has His timescale. His plans are perfect. Christ's friends will know everlasting joy—and Christ's enemies will surely 'bite the dust'.

Another one bites the dust

The Lord will come and not be slow;
His footsteps cannot err;
Before Him righteousness shall go,
His royal harbinger.

Mercy and truth, that long were missed,
Now joyfully are met;
Sweet peace and righteousness have kissed,
And hand in hand are set.

(John Milton, 1608–74)

9

Don't let the sun go down on your anger

I travelled home from a church meeting once with a Christian gentleman who had been married for more years than I had been alive. He revealed that while his marriage inevitably had its ups and downs, he and his wife aspired to hold to the motto, 'Do not let the sun go down on your anger.' That is, if there were any tensions or arguments between them, they had to be resolved before the day was done. The motto is a good one for married couples, I'm sure.

The expression 'Don't let the sun go down on your anger' originates from Paul's letter to some Christians based at Ephesus. In Ephesians 4:26,27 we read the exhortation '"Be angry, and do not sin": do not let the sun go down on your wrath, nor give place to the devil.'

Anger is like fire. It can have a destructive or a constructive use. Fire can boil water and heat the house—but fire can also destroy a property. Anger can sometimes get things done. Presumably it was William Wilberforce's anger at the injustices of slavery which led, successfully, to his campaigning for its removal. And it might be a local community's anger over the lack of road safety which leads to getting a pedestrian crossing installed near a school. Yet anger, when uncontrolled, is very destructive. It can lead even to murder. On a humorous note it has been well said that 'letting off steam can get you into hot water', and 'You don't get rid of your temper by losing it'.

It is quite possible that Paul had Psalm 4:4 in mind when he advised, 'Do not let the sun go down on your wrath.' Psalm 4:4 makes the point that you are to 'Be angry, and do not sin. Meditate within your heart on your bed, and be still.' Anger in itself is not necessarily sinful, for the Bible reveals that the God of the Old Testament and the Lord Jesus in the New Testament both expressed anger. Their anger, though, was a holy, sinless anger—a righteous indignation. It is possible, therefore, to be angry and not to sin, but we have to confess that this is a rare occurrence in fallen human beings such as we are. Our anger can be triggered by an affront to our pride or by personal pique. It can then fester and lead, if we are not careful, to cynicism, malice, rage and the desire for revenge. It can—as Paul suggests in our verses—give an opportunity to the devil or a foothold for Satan's ravaging work. So Paul exhorts: '"Be angry, and do not sin": do not let the sun go down on your wrath, nor give place to the devil.'

Paul's inspired words were addressed first of all to believers within the Christian community. The Christian gospel is a gospel of reconciliation. Paul had already explained that 'now in Christ Jesus you who once were far off have been brought near by the blood of Christ' (Eph. 2:13). It is highly hypocritical, therefore, for one Christian to be alienated from another, hence we are obliged to do all within our power to seek harmonious relations with our brothers and sisters in Christ and to deal with any causes of hostility and alienation. The Lord Jesus once said, 'Therefore if you bring your gift to the altar, and there remember that your brother has something against you, leave your gift there before the altar, and go your way. First be reconciled to your brother, and then come and offer your gift' (Matt. 5:23-24). Our fellowship—or lack of it—with our fellow believers on the horizontal level affects our fellowship with our God on the vertical level.

'Be angry, and do not sin.' Personally, I don't think that a fallen human being can be angry without sinning. Hence it is best not to be angry at all, or, if we are, to deal with it before God straight away and leave the cause of our anger with Him. This is more than a personal opinion, as Scripture seems to bear this out:

'*He who is* slow to wrath has great understanding, but *he who is* impulsive exalts folly' (Prov. 14:29).

'A quick-tempered *man* acts foolishly, and a man of wicked intentions is hated' (Prov. 14:17).

'A wrathful man stirs up strife, but *he who is* slow to anger allays contention' (Prov. 15:18).

'*He who is* slow to anger *is* better than the mighty, and he who rules his spirit than he who takes a city' (Prov. 16:32).

'Do not hasten in your spirit to be angry, for anger rests in the bosom of fools' (Eccles. 7:9).

So we must seek God's grace to control our anger, if we are given to anger—and who isn't prone to this when under the right provocation? Which one of us isn't a walking time bomb when it comes to anger? Centuries ago, Aristotle was most astute when he said, 'Anyone can become angry ... But to be angry with the right person, to the right degree, at the right time, for the right purpose and in the right way—this is not easy.'

Thankfully, the Christian life begins and ends with the saving grace of God in Christ—His love to the undeserving. And thankfully, too, the Christian life is a life empowered by the Holy Spirit of God. Galatians 5:22-23 states that 'the fruit of the Spirit is love, joy, peace, longsuffering, kindness, goodness, faithfulness, gentleness, self-control.'

Our fits of temper apart, then, by the sanctifying grace of God and by the Spirit of God, we can yet be the people God would have us be.

10

Flat on your face

'I fell flat on my face.' We use this expression in both a literal and a figurative way. Both, however, involve degrees of embarrassment and humiliation.

When I was out running not so long ago, I tripped over some uneven paving stones near a bus stop. I pitched forward and fell flat on my face in front of a row of bus travellers. I suffered some cuts and bruises, but the feeling of humiliation in front of all those spectators hurt even more.

Then there are times when we attempt something with confidence and high hopes, but fail and disappoint ourselves. On such occasions we might be heard to utter, 'I set out in good faith, but fell flat on my face.'

The expression 'to fall on one's face' is actually an expression which is biblical in its origin. In the time of Moses, there lived a prophet of dubious reputation by the name of Balaam. Balaam set out to curse the people of Israel, but was prevented from so doing by 'the angel of the LORD'—possibly a pre-incarnate appearance of the Lord Jesus Christ. Numbers 22:31 records 'Then the LORD opened Balaam's eyes, and he saw the Angel of the LORD standing in the way with His drawn sword in His hand; and he bowed his head and *fell flat on his face.*' In Numbers 16:4 we also read that 'Moses ... fell on his face' when a man called Korah falsely accused him of unjustly lording it over the people. Then, when we turn to the New Testament, we see that when John the apostle glimpsed the Lord Jesus in all His risen, ascended, glorified majesty, he 'fell at His feet as dead' (Rev. 1:17).

So we are concerned with this expression 'to fall on one's face'. Are there any spiritual lessons to be gleaned from this expression? Yes, there are.

Lessons in Worship

Truth be told, before Almighty God, our rightful place can only be flat on our faces in the dust. He alone is supremely great. He alone is worthy of our absolute and total allegiance and obedience. 'God is a spirit, infinite, eternal and unchangeable in His being, wisdom, power, holiness, justice, goodness and truth.'[1]

God alone is God. He is incomparable, sovereign and supreme. He has no rivals and He tolerates no rivals. He is the greatest and best of all beings—our Maker, Sustainer, Governor and King. Reverence becomes Him. Worship is due to Him. Our place before Him is flat on our faces. We are creatures—He is our Creator. We are sinners—He is our Saviour. We are subjects—He is our King. 'Oh come, let us worship and bow down; let us kneel before the LORD our Maker. For He *is* our God, and we *are* the people of His pasture, and the sheep of His hand' (Ps. 95:6-7).

Interestingly, when we turn our thoughts to the New Testament, the Greek word used for worship is 'proskuneo'. This means 'to bow down, to bend the knee, to fall at another's feet'.

Lessons in Sanctification

Falling flat on our faces, in the figurative sense, can hurt. No one in his right mind enjoys failure. No one has cause to be proud of his folly and mistakes and the consequences that have to be faced. Yet such things can be made useful to us and draw us

---

1. This description is from the *Westminster Shorter Catechism*, the answer to Question 4.

closer to our Saviour. Jesus described Himself as 'gentle and lowly in heart' (Matt. 11:29).

Experiences that humiliate us can smooth off our rough edges and make us more like Jesus—drawing us closer to Him for mercy and grace. Our Father in heaven has His way of knocking the pride and self-sufficiency out of us! The Scripture says that '*God resists the proud, but gives grace to the humble*' (James 4:6). Hence the Psalmist could testify, 'It is good for me that I have been afflicted, that I may learn Your statutes.' (Ps. 119:71).

In John Bunyan's *Pilgrim's Progress* Part II, we are taken on a very instructive visit to 'The Valley of Humiliation'. Every Christian will surely visit this valley. It would be a place to fear and dread were it not for the blessing of God. In this valley—the valley of failure, loss and disappointment—the Lord draws near to us in a special way. The blessing of this valley is thus known to believers alone. Let us quote from *Pilgrim's Progress*:

> This Valley of Humiliation is of itself as fruitful a place, as any the crow flies over ... Behold how green this Valley is, also how beautified with lilies ...
>
> In this Valley our Lord formerly had His country house, He loved much to be here: He loved also to walk in these meadows, for He found the air was pleasant: Besides, here a man shall be free from the noise and from the hurrying of this life: all states are full of noise and confusion, only the Valley of Humiliation is that empty and solitary place. Here a man shall not be so let and hindered in his contemplation, as in other places he is apt to be. This is a Valley that nobody walks in, but those that love a Pilgrim's life;—and though Christian had the hard hap to meet here with Apollyon, and to enter with him a brisk encounter, yet I must tell you, that in former times,

men have met with angels here, have found pearls here and have in this place found the Words of Life.

Did I say our Lord had here in former days His country house and that He loved here to walk? I will add, in this place, and to the people that live and trace these grounds, He has left a yearly revenue to be faithfully paid there at certain seasons for their maintenance by the way, and for their farther encouragement to go on their Pilgrimage.[2]

'I fell flat on my face.' Ouch! But here is a reminder of our true position and place before Almighty God. And here is a place and means of spiritual blessing, drawing us nearer to the crucified Christ and the God who is the fount of every blessing.

We will all surely fall flat on our faces sometime. It's a law of life. When you next find yourself flat on your face, try and remember the following lines from *Pilgrim's Progress*:

> He that is down, needs fear no fall
> He that is low no pride
> He that is humble, ever shall
> Have God to be his Guide.

(John Bunyan, 1628–88)

---

2. *Pilgrim's Progress,* Part 2, Banner of Truth, 1977, reprinted from 1895 edition, pp. 281, 282.

11

God willing

'See you next week, God willing.' The expression 'God willing' is confined to Christian circles—and even within Christian circles, its use tends to be confined to the more devout. In the Arab-speaking world, however, the words 'insha'allah' can often be heard. These words similarly mean 'If God wills'.

The expression 'God willing' derives from the Bible both generally and specifically. Throughout the Bible's pages generally, we read of the absolute and total sovereignty of Almighty God—that is that *He* is the One in control of the universe which He has created. A consequence of God's sovereignty is His providence. God's providence means that all that ever happens in the universe is ultimately due to His will and direction. 'For of Him and through Him and to Him *are* all things, to whom *be* glory forever. Amen' (Rom. 11:36).

The *Westminster Shorter Catechism* encapsulates the teaching of the Bible when it states:

'The decrees of God are His eternal purpose, according to the counsel of His will, whereby, for His own glory, He hath foreordained whatsoever comes to pass'(Q.7).

'God's works of providence are His most holy, wise and powerful preserving and governing all His creatures and all their actions' (Q.11).

Specifically, however, the expression 'God willing' comes to us directly from the pages of the Bible, for in James 4:13-16 we read: 'Come now, you who say, "Today or tomorrow we will go to such and such a city, spend a year there, buy and sell, and make a profit"; whereas you do not know what *will happen* tomorrow. For what *is* your life? It is even a vapor that appears for a little time and then vanishes away. Instead you *ought* to say, "*If the Lord wills*, we shall live and do this or that." But now you boast in your arrogance. All such boasting is evil.'

When we use the expression 'God willing', we are acknowledging that we ourselves are not in charge of our lives, but rather that Almighty God is. All of our earthly plans, hopes, ambitions and aspirations are subject to His will. It is believed that Thomas A Kempis used to say, 'Man proposes, but God disposes.' We do not know what might happen tomorrow, next week, next month or next year. But God does. He does so because He is already there and has already foreordained what will happen then. When we make our plans, therefore, it is wise to say, 'God willing'—for God might have other purposes, and we do not have His foresight. Our plans may have to be altered—ill health, personal calamity or even death may intervene to accommodate God's purposes. Hence Proverbs 27:1 is so pertinent: 'Do not boast about tomorrow, for you do not know what a day may bring forth.'

'God willing.' Ultimately, the reason for everything is the sovereign will of God. It is our bounden duty to submit to this without murmuring. His ways are best, for He is surely too wise to make mistakes and too loving to be unkind. When our plans are altered, therefore, and when our hopes and aspirations are frustrated and disappointed, the will of God is our resting place. Our Father in heaven knows what is best for His children. He knows what is best for us far better than we ourselves know. Hence the strong application of Romans 8:28: 'And we know that all things work together for good to those who love God, to those who are the called according to *His* purpose.'

'God willing.' The Lord Jesus taught us to pray to God, 'Thy will be done.' This is a petition that we will know, obey and submit to the will of God in all things. Submission to the will of God is surely the secret of Christian contentment. We may safely trust the wisdom of the circumstances which God sees fit to send our way. It has been well said that those who see the hand of God in everything can safely leave everything in the hand of God. The will of God is described in the Bible as 'good and acceptable and perfect' (Rom. 12:2). The very best cannot be bettered!

Thou sweet, beloved will of God,
My anchor ground, my fortress hill,
My spirit's silent, fair abode,
In Thee I hide me and am still.

O Will, that willest good alone,
Lead Thou the way, Thou guidest best;
A little child, I follow on,
And, trusting, lean upon Thy breast.

Oh lightest burden, sweetest yoke;
It lifts, it bears my happy soul,
It giveth wings to this poor heart;
My freedom is Thy good control.

Upon God's will I lay me down,
As child upon its mother's breast;
No silken couch, nor softest bed,
Could ever give me such deep rest.

Thou wonderful grand will, my God,
With triumph now I make it mine;
And faith shall cry a joyous Yes
To every dear command of Thine.

(Gerhardt Tersteegen, 1697–1769)
(Translated by Jean Sophia Pigott, 1845–1882)

12

Hiding your light under a bushel

'You've been hiding your light under a bushel!' You hear this remark occasionally in the secular world, when people reveal they have talents we hadn't known about. The expression was uttered in my office coming up to Christmas-time. Volunteers were needed for a carol concert, and it came to light that some could play the guitar, others were adept on the piano and yet others had quite passable singing voices. Musical talent is not a part of our day-to-day job description. Thus these abilities were hidden until then—they were 'a light under a bushel'.

A 'bushel' refers to a basket or measuring bowl for wheat or other grain, which was used in Bible times. The expression concerning 'hiding one's light under a bushel' actually originates from the lips of none less than the Lord Jesus Christ and He used it on more than one occasion. In His well-known Sermon on the Mount, for instance, He uttered the following words to Christians of all eras:

> You are the light of the world. A city that is set on a hill cannot be hidden. *Nor do they light a lamp and put it under a basket, but on a lampstand*, and it gives light to all *who are* in the house. Let your light so shine before men, that they may see your good works and glorify your Father in heaven (Matt. 5:14-16).

Christian Witness

This expression about 'hiding a light under a bushel' was originally to do with a Christian's witness in the secular world. While there is a private facet to the Christian faith—there is a vital place for private prayer and communion with God and meditating on His Word—Christianity is more than something confined to a Christian's private life. Jesus exhorts His followers to shine out for Him in public. Christians are to manifest their salvation from Monday to Saturday, outside of church, as well as joining in public worship inside church on a Sunday. The salvation Christ has procured for us is to be manifested in every area of our lives—how we think; how we speak; how we don't speak, what we do; what we don't do; how we behave, act and react. There is, and there is to be, no corner of our lives which is exempt from Christ's absolute claim.

'You are the light of the world,' says the Lord Jesus to His followers. Of course, a Christian's light is not something intrinsic to himself or herself as an individual. By nature we are in spiritual darkness. Salvation, however, entails coming to the light of Christ, and this dispels our spiritual darkness. Salvation is a gracious work of the Triune God: 'For it is the God who commanded light to shine out of darkness who has shone in our hearts to *give* the light of the knowledge of the glory of God in the face of Jesus Christ' (2 Cor. 4:6). A Christian's light, therefore, is not an intrinsic light but a reflected light—a result of belonging to the One who affirmed, 'I am the light of the world. He who follows Me shall not walk in darkness, but have the light of life' (John 8:12).

Shining for Jesus, therefore, is really just a matter of being who we are in Christ. If we truly *know* His salvation, we will *show* His salvation. And the whole New Testament exhorts us to live for Christ and neither hide nor tarnish the light we have received, whether by cowardice or indifference to the need of others who are heading for the darkness of a Christless hell. Hence Paul enjoins believers in Ephesians 5:8 'For you were once darkness, but now *you are* light in the Lord. Walk as children of light' and in Philippians 2:15 to become 'blameless and harmless, children of God without fault in the midst of a crooked and perverse generation, among whom you shine as lights in the world.'

Shining for Christ

If we are Christians, each of us has a calling to shine for Jesus— to reflect the fact that we are recipients of the special favour of God in Christ. God's providence puts us in certain places so that we may be a testimony to His saving grace there. If we belong to Jesus, He says that we are the light of the world. And if we belong to Jesus, we are called to be lights in a dark world— to reflect and share the love and light of Christ which we have received. Not to do so is akin to 'hiding our light under a bushel'. Light is to shine out, and not be covered over, if it is to prevent people from stumbling in the dark. So Jesus said, and still says, 'No one, when he has lit a lamp, puts *it* in a secret place or under a basket, but on a lampstand, that those who come in may see the light' (Luke 11:33).

Who knows what God may yet do through you for the blessing of others if you allow Him to reflect and radiate the light of Christ through you? Remember what Jesus said: 'Let your light so shine before men, that they may see your good works and glorify your Father in heaven' (Matt. 5:16). This is an apt hymn for children of all ages in its words:

A Pinch of Salt

Jesus bids us shine with a pure, clear light,
Like a little candle burning in the night.
In this world of darkness, so let us shine,
You in your small corner, and I in mine.

Jesus bids us shine, first of all for Him;
Well He sees and knows it, if our light grows dim:
He looks down from Heaven to see us shine,
You in your small corner, and I in mine.

Jesus bids us shine, then, for all around,
Many kinds of darkness in the world are found:
Sin and want and sorrow; so we must shine,
You in your small corner, and I in mine.

(Susan B. Warner, published 1864)

13

I wash my hands of the matter

To 'wash one's hands of a matter' refers popularly to the wish to have nothing to do with something or of abdicating all responsibility for something. The expression suggests you are 'clean' of a matter and not stained and soiled with 'guilt on your hands'. An exasperated parent may thus threaten a rebellious teenager with the words 'I'm sick and tired of telling you to do your homework. I won't tell you again. Now it's up to you whether you pass or fail your exams. I wash my hands of you.'

The expression 'to wash your hands of the matter' originates from the trial of the Lord Jesus Christ. The Jewish authorities were anxious to put Jesus to death, but lacked the authority to do so. Such authority was vested in the Roman government of the day, specifically in Pontius Pilate, the Roman governor. Pilate personally did not wish to see Jesus crucified, as he knew He was guilty of no crime. But Pilate caved in to the popular demand. With Pilate wishing to exonerate himself, the Bible records when he 'saw that he could not prevail at all, but rather *that* a tumult was rising, he took water and washed *his* hands before the multitude, saying, "I am innocent of the blood of this just Person. You see *to it*."...and when he had scourged Jesus, he delivered Him to be crucified' (Matt. 27:24, 26).

Pilate here comes over as a somewhat cowardly man, one lacking the courage of his convictions. He 'washed his hands' of Jesus, symbolically protesting he was innocent of His murder. Yet his protest was merely symbolic and not actual. He could have prevented Jesus' crucifixion, but didn't. If the Jews had rioted, the Emperor just might have removed Pilate from office for failing to keep order. Pilate thus looked after his own interests and succumbed to popular demand for Jesus' crucifixion. In so doing he kept in with both the Jews and the Emperor, and gained an infamous place in world history.

Are there any spiritual lessons to be gained from Pilate's famous 'washing of his hands'? Yes, there are.

The Relevance

Pontius Pilate was the Roman governor or 'Procurator' in Judea from A.D. 26-37. The evidence for this is found both inside and outside the Bible. Pilate was a contemporary of the Son of God and he held office during that epochal time of world history.

Pilate reminds us of the historical reality of the Christian faith. The saving acts of God in Christ actually occurred in time and space. The Christian faith is no mere artistic invention but a matter of historical truth. Christianity is based on historical facts, not mythological fables. Peter wrote, 'For we did not follow cunningly devised fables when we made known to you the power and coming of our Lord Jesus Christ, but were eyewitnesses of His majesty' (2 Pet. 1:16).

The Innocence

Both Pilate and his wife were convinced of the absolute innocence of the Lord Jesus. He had committed no crime deserving of capital punishment. Even so, Pilate sentenced Him to death. Pilate's wife said to him, 'Have nothing to do with that just Man, for I have suffered many things today in a dream because of Him' (Matt. 27:19). Pilate himself protested to the Jews, 'Why, what evil has He done?' (Matt. 27:23) and 'I find no fault in Him *at all*' (John 18:38). This raises the question: Why, then, was Jesus put to death? Because of Pilate's weakness? Yes. But the deeper reason, according to the Bible, is that Jesus died not for His own sins, for He had none. He died for the sins of others. He died as the substitute for sinners to save them from the wrath of God which is their just due. It is because Jesus died in the place of sinners that God is able both to punish sin and to pardon those who believe—to be just and to justify all who put their faith in Jesus. The substitutionary death of Jesus at Calvary takes us to the very heart of the gospel: He 'was delivered up because of *our* offenses' (Rom. 4:25). 'He *was* wounded for *our* transgressions' (Isa. 53:5).

The Providence

Lastly, Pontius Pilate's hand-washing informs us of the absolute sovereignty of God and His all-embracing providence. God has His eternal plan of salvation to save a people for Himself and for His glory. Central to this plan is the atoning sacrifice of Christ at Calvary. How did God actually execute His plan in time and space? It was through the instrumentality of Pontius Pilate. God's providence ensured that Jesus would die at Calvary. Calvary was ultimately His act. Even human wickedness—the malice of the mob and the weakness of Pilate—was woven into serving God's greater purpose. It was the wickedness of man which brought the blessing of God. Jesus was 'delivered by the determined purpose and foreknowledge of God', and 'by lawless hands [was] …put to death' (see Acts 2:23). Even the wickedest enemies of God are actually only axes, saws and hammers in the divine hands. Like Judas Iscariot, they are ignorantly God's instruments for doing His work and will in the world.

This was most certainly the case when Pontius Pilate 'washed his hands' of Jesus and handed Him over to be crucified.

'I wash my hands of the matter.' The expression is a biblical one. It takes us back to the momentous time in history when Jesus was condemned to death of the cross. It reminds us that the Christian faith is an historical faith—here we are dealing with reality. It reminds us of the sinlessness of Jesus—'Christ died for *our* sins' (1 Cor. 15:3). It encourages us with the truth that whatever is going on in our tumultuous world, our God is always in control. He 'works all things according to the counsel of His will' (Eph. 1:11).

This is my Father's world:
O let me ne'er forget
That though the wrong seems oft so strong,
God is the ruler yet.

(Maltbie Davenport Babcock)

14

It takes all sorts

'It takes all sorts.' This expression was sometimes heard in a railway office in which I once worked. We were an exceedingly diverse workforce. I used to sit opposite a Muslim lady, and we got on quite well. One or two members of the workforce weren't long out of college, yet there was also an ex-army man, who had 'been there, seen it and done it'. One or two male colleagues were real railway buffs—their work was their hobby as well as their living. Another man kept reptiles. My main hobby was as it still is—running. The colourful characters working for the railways sometimes made me feel rather ordinary—but 'it takes all sorts'.

The Disciples: Diversity in Unity

If it takes all sorts to make a world, the Bible reveals that it also takes all sorts to make up the church of Christ. The Lord Jesus initially chose twelve disciples, and these too were very diverse characters. Peter was somewhat impetuous. Andrew, his brother, was a quieter man, yet possessed of the gift of gentle persuasion. Thomas was somewhat morose by nature. James and John were fishermen, and Matthew was originally a tax collector—in league with Rome, the foreign, occupying power. Simon the Zealot and Judas Iscariot, however, were Jewish nationalists, all for overthrowing Rome by military—or paramilitary—force. The table talk of these disciples therefore must have been very interesting, and no doubt sometimes became heated. The disciples were diverse, and yet they were all one in their friendship with Jesus. He had called them. He eventually transformed them. They became ambassadors for Christ. They were forged into being fearless evangelists and compassionate pastors of Christ's flock. John, the one-time fisherman, eventually wrote an incomparable Gospel—the Gospel of John—an account of Jesus' sayings and signs, proving to the world that Jesus is the Christ, the Son of God, and that eternal life is found by believing in Him. The grace of God in Christ brought out abilities John never knew he had.

The Church: Diversity in Unity

Interestingly, in the New Testament, the apostle Paul likens the church of Christ to the human body, with Christ as its head. The human body is also both diverse and yet one. And so Paul writes in Romans 12:4-6: 'For as we have many members in one body, but all the members do not have the same function, so we, *being* many, are one body in Christ, and individually members of one another. Having then gifts differing according to the grace that is given to us, *let us use them*...' Then, in 1 Corinthians 12:14-17, he writes, 'For in fact the body is not one member but many. If the foot should say, "Because I am not a hand, I am not of the body," is it therefore not of the body? And if the ear should say, "Because I am not an eye, I am not of the body," is it therefore not of the body? If the whole body *were* an eye, where *would be* the hearing? If the whole *were* hearing, where *would be* the smelling?'

Individual Fingerprints

What is Paul saying? He is enjoining us to respect our individuality and be the unique people God has created us to be. We all have a particular role and function in the greater plan of God. True happiness consists in finding the role and function for which we have been designed by God and then fulfilling that role and function to His praise and glory. In the church of the Lord Jesus Christ, every single individual has a niche—and has a particular part to play. Every single individual, not just the church leaders, has a sphere of service. God saves us for a purpose. Ephesians 2:10 states: 'For we are His workmanship, created in Christ Jesus for good works, which God prepared beforehand that we should walk in them.' 1 Peter 4:10-11 exhorts believers in these words: 'As each one has received a gift, minister it to one another, as good stewards of the manifold grace of God. If anyone speaks, *let him speak* as the oracles of God. If anyone ministers, *let him do it* as with the ability which God supplies, that in all things God may be glorified through Jesus Christ, to whom belong the glory and the dominion forever and ever. Amen.'

It Takes All Sorts

So 'it takes all sorts to make a world.' Paradoxically, the expression is not found in the Bible, and yet the diversity of the church, the body of Christ, shows that the expression is distinctly biblical. You are the only you! So, seek to be the person God made you to be. Seek to fulfil the unique function God has for you—nothing more, nothing less and nothing else. Anything less will only lead to frustration.

> There's a work for Jesus,
> Ready at your hand,
> 'Tis a task the Master
> Just for you has planned.
> Haste to do His bidding,
> Yield Him service true;
> There's a work for Jesus
> None but you can do.
>
> (Elsie D. Yale, 1912)

15

It wasn't done in a corner

Occasionally, certain events receive media saturation and grab the public attention. Examples include a general election, a sporting event like the Olympics or soccer world cup, or even, sadly, a celebrity scandal. When these occur, a conversation might go 'Have you heard about ...?' The answer might be something like 'I could hardly not hear of it. It wasn't exactly done in a corner.'

The expression 'It wasn't done in a corner' refers to an event that has become well known, and has been broadcast and become common knowledge. A synonymous expression might be 'It is no secret.' But where does the expression 'It wasn't done in a corner' come from? It comes from the Bible.

The apostle Paul's love for Jesus and his zeal for the gospel often got him into trouble. Acts 25 and 26 relate one of the occasions when he had been arrested and was on trial for his Christian faith. He used the opportunity before King Agrippa and Governor Festus to bear witness to Christ—to testify what He had done for him and what He could do for others. Oddly, although it was Paul who was on trial before Agrippa and Festus, when we read the account we get the sense that ultimately it was Agrippa and Festus themselves who were on trail, and that they were not on trial before Paul, but before Almighty God Himself. When Paul had concluded his testimony, Luke informs us that

> Now as he thus made his defense, Festus said with a loud voice, 'Paul, you are beside yourself! Much learning is driving you mad!'

But he said, 'I am not mad, most noble Festus, but speak the words of truth and reason. For the king, before whom I also speak freely, knows these things; for I am convinced that none of these things escapes his attention, *since this thing was not done in a corner.*' (Acts 26:24-26).

'This thing was not done in a corner.' Paul was saying that the gospel of Christ had become well known throughout the Roman Empire, and that it was incumbent on those who had heard it to act upon it, if they valued their souls. 'A prudent *man* foresees evil and hides himself, but the simple pass on and are punished' (Prov. 22:3).

The Christian faith is an evangelistic faith. Good news is for sharing. The gospel has been broadcast, and the gospel is to be broadcast until the time Jesus comes again. Jesus' parting words were a command: 'Go into all the world and preach the gospel ...' (Mark 16:15). The good news is that Jesus saves. We have need of a Saviour, and in the crucified Christ we find the Saviour for our deepest need.

When we hear this good news, it is incumbent on us to act on it. Indeed, God will hold us accountable for how we act, or do not act, on it. Every single person who has ever lived will be judged on the light that he or she has received—Agrippa, Festus, you and I. If we know that we are sinners under divine judgement, and if we know that Jesus is the only Saviour, woe betide us if we don't cleave to Him as our own personal Saviour!

Here in the 'Christian West' where there is gospel liberty, we will have no excuse. In the providence of God we still have liberty to preach and hear the gospel—from the pulpit in churches and mission halls, over the airwaves, over the Internet, and in the open air by both verbal proclamation and printed pages. We are privileged, but with privilege comes responsibility. 'For everyone to whom much is given, from him much will be required' (Luke 12:48). Jesus said, 'And that servant who knew his master's will, and did not prepare *himself* or do according to his will, shall be beaten with many *stripes*' (Luke 12:47). But what of those nations which are closed to the gospel? What of those who genuinely have never heard of the Saviour who saves and necessity of believing in Him? We leave this matter in the hands of God. 'Shall not the Judge of all the earth do right?' (Gen. 18:25). 'But he who did not know, yet committed things deserving of stripes, shall be beaten with few' (Luke 12:48).

'This thing was not done in a corner.' Agrippa and Festus knew—Paul knew—all knew the gospel. And they knew that Paul knew. Yet, sadly, they did not act on it. Agrippa stifled his conscience and said dismissively to Paul, 'You almost persuade me to become a Christian' (Acts 26:28). But as one person said, 'He who is almost persuaded is almost saved, and to be almost saved is to be entirely lost.'[1] When it comes to the matter of our eternal salvation the Bible marks things out in black and white, as the two following verses clearly state:

'He who believes in the Son has everlasting life; and he who does not believe the Son shall not see life, but the wrath of God abides on him' (John 3:36).

'And this is the testimony: that God has given us eternal life, and this life is in His Son. He who has the Son has life; he who does not have the Son of God does not have life' (1 John 5:11,12).

---

1. A saying attributed to Rev Brundage, taken up by Philip P Bliss (who was in the congregation) in the hymn 'Almost Persuaded', John Julian, Dictionary of Hymnology, 1907.

16

Just an empty shibboleth

One dictionary defines a 'Shibboleth' as a 'catchword, (esp. outworn or empty) formula etc., insisted on by a group.' A shibboleth, therefore, refers to words which are used to show we belong to a particular 'in' group. The group could be our peers at school, a work group, or a political or sporting club. Sadly, shibboleths can also be unofficially insisted on if we wish to gain acceptance in certain Christian circles.

Shibboleths are often regarded as referring to words which are largely empty of meaning. They just roll off the tongue without any thought. Here, then, we are in the realms of the platitude, cliché and jargon. We have all been served in a fast-food restaurant by a stressed assistant who tells us to 'Enjoy your meal'—giving the impression that the person serving us does not really mean it, but has been told to say it. The same is true of those utility call centres which close each call by telling us to 'Have a nice day.' More serious in this regard are those Christian leaders who state publically that they do not believe in the fundamentals of the faith they have been ordained to uphold, but still stand up on a Sunday and recite the Apostles' Creed with its affirmation that Christ was 'conceived by the Holy Spirit ... and rose again on the third day.'

Origins in the Bible
The Hebrew word 'shibboleth' means 'grains of wheat'. The use of the word to distinguish one group from another takes us way back to the time of the Judges in the Promised Land. The book of Judges is set in a time of spiritual declension, after the Exodus

71

from Egypt, but before the kingship was established in Israel. Sadly, there was an internal feud between the tribe of Ephraim and the warriors of Gilead which saw Gilead defeating Ephraim and the surviving Ephraimites trying to cross the River Jordan to get back home. The Gileadites, however, set up a sentry at a ford there, and they identified the Ephraimites by their ability—or lack of ability—to pronounce the word 'shibboleth'—for they could not pronounce the sound 'sh' but only 'ss'. The account records:

> The Gileadites seized the fords of the Jordan before the Ephraimites *arrived*. And when *any* Ephraimite who escaped said, 'Let me cross over,' the men of Gilead would say to him, '*Are* you an Ephraimite?' If he said, 'No,' then they would say to him, 'Then say, "Shibboleth"!' And he would say, 'Sibboleth,' for he could not pronounce *it* right. Then they would take him and kill him at the fords of the Jordan. There fell at that time forty-two thousand Ephraimites (Judg. 12:5-6).

So the Ephraimites then fatally failed the pronunciation test of 'shibboleth' before the Gileadite warriors. From this originates the word 'shibboleth' as referring to a kind of password to give access and acceptance in particular spheres. But what is the application and relevance of this word which few know actually comes from a book set in the early years of Old Testament history?

Shibboleths Warn us Against a Merely Nominal Faith

The true Christian faith, that is, knowing the salvation of God in Christ, certainly involves a right confession with our mouths—yet it is also far more than that. In Romans 10:9 Paul writes that 'if you confess with your mouth the Lord Jesus *and believe in your heart* that God has raised Him from the dead, you will be saved.'

This 'heart work' nurtured in us by God's Holy Spirit always takes precedence. The confession with the mouth is the fruit of the root. If there is no 'heart work', the fruit is artificial—a mere shibboleth. 'For with the heart one believes unto righteousness, and with the mouth confession is made unto salvation' (Rom. 10:10). Paul, here, was confident that a genuine work of grace had been performed by God in the hearts of his readers, for he had previously written, 'But God be thanked that *though* you were slaves of sin, yet you obeyed from the heart that form of doctrine to which you were delivered' (Rom. 6:17). So apart from a 'heart work' any Christian profession will surely be an empty shibboleth—words without reality. Such is unequivocally condemned by the Lord Jesus as religious hypocrisy. Quoting from Isaiah the prophet, He condemned the religious leaders of His day with the words of God: 'These people draw near to Me with their mouth, and honor Me with their lips, but their heart is far from Me' (Matt. 15:8). Shibboleths therefore warn us against holding a merely nominal, 'lip service' kind of faith.

Shibboleths Are a Warning to Christians

A daily time and routine for prayer—communion with God and laying out our lives before Him—is essential for our Christian well-being. But prayer must never become a routine. Routine is good, but it can have the danger of degenerating into a mere ritual of 'saying our prayers'. Prayer is not a matter of reciting a formula, but it is a relationship—talking to, and being silent before, the living God.

> Prayer is a form of communication between God and ourselves by which we set before Him our desires, our joys, our complaints—in short, all that goes on in our heart.

This being so, every time we call on the Lord we should be careful to descent into the depth of our heart and to speak to Him from there, and not just with the throat or tongue.[1]

The Lord Jesus, knowing the pitfalls into which our prayer lives may fall, gave a warning which is perennially relevant: 'And when you pray, do not use vain repetitions as the heathen *do.* For they think that they will be heard for their many words' (Matt. 6:7).

Empty Shibboleths

'It's just an empty shibboleth ...' Words without reality. We often hear them, but are we guilty of saying them ourselves. Jesus said, 'Not everyone who says to Me, "Lord, Lord," shall enter the kingdom of heaven, but he who does the will of My Father in heaven.' (Matt. 7:21). May the Lord save us from a merely nominal religion! And may the Lord enable us to pray with sincerity and reality, and an earnest desire for His glory.

> I often say my prayers
> But do I ever pray?
> And do the wishes of my heart
> Go with the words I say?
>
> I may as well kneel down
> And worship gods of stone,
> As offer to the living God
> A prayer of words alone.
>
> For words without the heart
> The Lord will never hear,
> Nor will He to those lips attend
> Whose prayers are not sincere.

1. John Calvin (trans. Stuart Olyott), *Truth for all Time,* Edinburgh, Banner of Truth 1998, p. 51.

Just an empty shibboleth

Lord teach me what I need,
And teach me how to pray;
Nor let me ask Thy grace
Not felling what I say

(John Burton, 1803–77)

17

Laughter is the best medicine

'Laughter is the best medicine.' The expression is difficult to prove. A few years ago there was a film, purportedly based on real life, about a trainee doctor who was convinced that the saying was true. The film was entitled *Patch Adams.* The doctor in question got into hot water with the medical authorities, who accused him of mistaking his career as a doctor for a career as a comedian—turning the hospital ward into a theatre—believing that this would cure his patients.

'Laughter is the best medicine.' The saying is not found verbatim in the Bible, yet in the book of Proverbs we come very near to it. Proverbs 17:22 tells us that 'A merry heart does good, *like* medicine, but a broken spirit dries the bones.' Similarly, Proverbs 15:13 states that 'A merry heart makes a cheerful countenance, but by sorrow of the heart the spirit is broken.' The verses really just encapsulate what we very well know: it is good to have a laugh. Wholesome laughter is pleasant and acts as a tonic to the soul. Wholesome humour—being able to see the funny side of a situation—helps to oil the machinery of our lives, eases our load and brightens a dreary day. So thank God that He has given us a capacity for laughter and humour.

'A merry heart does good, *like* medicine...' Although it is pleasant to have a good laugh—and life would be somewhat colourless without humour—the Bible is justly not known for any kind of slapstick humour. There is a place for humour, but it is not in the Bible, for the Bible deals with the serious and solemn issues of eternity. The Bible tells of a heaven to be gained and a hell to be shunned. The Bible tells of a formidable God Whom we shall all have to face. Sniggering is out of place in the light of verses such as Hebrews 12:28-29: 'Therefore, since we are receiving a kingdom which cannot be shaken, let us have grace, by which we may serve God acceptably with reverence and godly fear. For our God *is* a consuming fire.' The good news, however, is that the Bible proclaims that there is a Saviour, Whose name is Jesus, and we can be eternally saved if we put our trust in Him.

Humour is undeniably pleasant—even if it can degenerate into something less than wholesome in a fallen world, tainted by sin. The danger of humour is that it can anaesthetise us from reality. The trivial can detract us from the crucial. Perhaps the writer of Ecclesiastes had this in mind when he wrote these difficult verses: 'Better to go to the house of mourning than to go to the house of feasting, for that *is* the end of all men; and the living will take *it* to heart. Sorrow *is* better than laughter, for by a sad countenance the heart is made better. The heart of the wise *is* in the house of mourning, but the heart of fools *is* in the house of mirth.' (Eccles. 7:2-4).

Holy Laughter?

Laughter, therefore, has its dangers and drawbacks. Hilarity can blind. Yet the Bible does reveal a phenomenon which we could term 'holy laughter'—a joy in the Lord which defies a frowning face. The people of Israel knew something of this when they returned to the Promised Land after their exile in Babylon. They testified that 'When the LORD brought back the captivity of Zion, we were like those who dream. Then our mouth was filled with laughter, and our tongue with singing. Then they said among the nations, "The LORD has done great things for them." The Lord has done great things for us, *and* we are glad' (Ps. 126:1-3).

We can argue here from the lesser to the greater—from the Old Testament to the New Testament. If the people of God in Old Testament times were glad and filled with laughter when the Lord brought them back to the land of Israel, what of the people of God in New Testament times—those living after Calvary and the empty tomb—on whom God has bestowed His saving grace and favour? Surely it is Christians alone who can truly say, 'The LORD has done great things for us, *and* we are glad.'

So the emphasis of the Bible is not so much on laughter as it is on joy—a joy in the Lord, irrespective of our earthly circumstances, which lasts for ever. Christians are not exhorted to be comedians, but they are exhorted to be joyful. 'Rejoice always' (1 Thess. 5:16). 'Rejoice in the Lord always. Again I will say, rejoice!' (Phil. 4:4). The clue to this last verse is on the very surface. Christian joy is peculiarly and specifically a joy 'in the Lord'. To expand this thought, it is a joy in the government and the grace of God.

We Rejoice in the Government of God

'The LORD has established His throne in heaven, and His kingdom rules over all' (Ps. 103:19). Our God reigns. Our Father is at the helm of the universe—in total and absolute control of the world generally, and the lives of His children particularly. He is too loving to be unkind, and too wise to make mistakes. Knowing that our lives are in His hand is surely a cause for comfort and joy. The Bible assures us that 'all things work together for good to those who love God, to those who are the called according to *His* purpose' (Rom. 8:28).

We Rejoice in the Grace of God

Could anything be more wonderful than being an object of the special grace of God? Yet every Christian has been singled out for blessing by God—an object of the favour of the Triune God. Every believer is 'elect according to the foreknowledge of God the Father, in sanctification of the Spirit, for obedience and sprinkling of the blood of Jesus Christ' (1 Pet. 1:2).

Why Almighty God should choose us for blessing—when all we deserve is His displeasure—is beyond us. But here is the wonder of grace—God's undeserved kindness and unmerited favour: in grace He gives us what we don't deserve; in mercy He doesn't give us what we do deserve. 'For by grace you have been saved through faith, and that not of yourselves; *it is* the gift of God, not of works, lest anyone should boast' (Eph. 2:8,9).

So there is a joy which is known to Christians alone—the joy of knowing God in Christ. Christians rejoice in a present salvation here, and Christians anticipate the fullness of this salvation hereafter. 'In Your presence *is* fullness of joy; at Your right hand *are* pleasures forevermore' (Ps. 16:11). Truly, in the memorable words of John Newton, 'Solid joys and lasting treasure, none but Zion's children know.'[1]

So is 'laughter the best medicine'? To a degree it is, for the Bible concurs that 'A merry heart does good, *like* medicine' (Prov. 17:22). But, this being said, we have to say that the laughter of the world is on a completely different planet from true Christian joy.

---

1. From Newton's hymn, 'Glorious Things of Thee Are Spoken'.

18

Out of the mouths of babes

'Out of the mouths of babes ...' We use this expression when young children say something which astonishes us. Or perhaps what they have said makes us laugh because of their honesty and innocent lack of discretion.

The story is told of a family who invited their minister and his wife to Sunday lunch. Wanting to do things the right way, the hostess—the mother—said to young John: 'Johnny, will you say the table grace for us?' A silence ensued, followed by a whispered question:

'Mummy, I don't know what to say.'

'Never mind,' answered his mother softly. 'Just say what Daddy said at the table this morning.'

'OK,' replied Johnny. 'Why did you have to invite those people to dinner today? Amen.'

'Out of the mouths of babes ...' The expression is used twice in the Bible, once in the Old Testament, and then quoted by the Lord Jesus in the New Testament.

Back to the Bible

Psalm 8 is a Psalm which extols both the glory and the grace of God. It begins thus: 'O Lord, our Lord, how excellent *is* Your name in all the earth' (Ps. 8:1) and goes on to marvel that this majestic God should ever take a loving interest in mortal human beings: 'What is man that You are mindful of him, and the son of man that You visit him?' (Ps. 8:4).

The expression under consideration is contained in verses 1b and 2 of Psalm 8: 'Who have set Your glory above the heavens!

Out of the mouth of babes and nursing infants You have ordained strength'—a passage that suggests that there are no age limits when it comes to the spiritual discernment of recognising the glory and greatness of God.

The verses of Psalm 8 are taken up by the Lord Jesus in an incident recorded in the New Testament in Matthew 21. It occurred during the last week of His earthly ministry, as He approached the cross of Calvary. He had entered Jerusalem triumphantly to public acclaim. He had cleansed the temple of abuses. He had performed miracles of healing on the blind and the lame. He certainly caused a stir!

So it was that children—either with true insight, or just repeating what they had heard others utter—cried out the Messianic acclamation: 'Hosanna to the Son of David!' (Matt. 21:15). At this, 'the chief priests and scribes ... were indignant; and said to Him, "Do You hear what these are saying?" And Jesus said to them, "Yes. Have you never read, 'Out of the mouth of babes and nursing infants You have perfected praise'?"' (see Matt. 21:15-16).

So the expression 'Out of the mouths of babes' has its ultimate reference point in the Lord Jesus Christ, when, to the indignation of the religious authorities, young children mouthed His praise. They cried to Him, 'Hosanna to the Son of David!' Their words were perhaps even more profound than they comprehended at that moment.

'Hosanna to the Son of David'

The word 'Hosanna' here is used—as it is today—in a worshipful way, as an address of praise. Mark's account of Jesus' triumphal entry into Jerusalem records that 'those who went before and those who followed cried out, 'Hosanna! "Blessed *is* He who comes in the name of the LORD!" Blessed *is* the kingdom of our father David that comes in the name of the LORD! Hosanna in the highest!' (Mark 11:9,10). As the Second Person of the blessed Trinity, it is right to offer praise to the Lord Jesus.

Originally, however, the word 'Hosanna' was a supplication rather than an address of praise. It was a cry to God meaning 'Save now'. Psalm 118:25 reads 'Save [lit. Hosanna] now, I pray, O LORD; O LORD, I pray, send now prosperity.' Here, the Lord Jesus is the answer to the Psalmist's plea, for His chief role and mission was to be the Saviour of sinners. 'The Son of Man has come to seek and to save that which was lost' (Luke 19:10). 'Christ Jesus came into the world to save sinners' (1 Tim. 1:15). This needed salvation was actually achieved less than a week after the children had cried 'Hosanna' to Jesus in the temple at Jerusalem. For it was now less than a week before Jesus would die on the cross to procure the eternal salvation of His people, and the age long cries of 'Hosanna' would be realised.

'Hosanna *to the Son of David'*

That the children address Jesus as the 'the Son of David' reveals a profound insight, for Jesus is indeed 'Great David's Greater Son'. The glorified Christ states in Revelation 22:16: 'I am the Root and the Offspring of David...'

Physically, Jesus was descended from David, as Matthew records at the start of his Gospel which begins, 'The book of the genealogy of Jesus Christ, the Son of David...' (Matt. 1:1) and traces Jesus' family tree through David's line. But more than this, the title 'Son of David' reveals Jesus to be the longed-for Messiah. David was Israel's greatest king. His rule was looked back on as something of a golden era. Scripture, however, describes Jesus as 'King of kings and Lord of lords' (Rev. 19:16). All kings possess both a kingdom and subjects. And it is the same with King Jesus. It is through Him that we enter the blessedness of the kingdom of heaven. Christ's office of King is a facet of His being the Messiah. As the Messiah, He combines the threefold role of prophet, priest and king in His one person.

The *Westminster Shorter Catechism* expresses this aspect of His work as King in these words: 'Christ executeth the office of a king in subduing us to Himself, in ruling and defending us and in restraining and conquering all His and our enemies.'[1]

> A king is a ruler of a kingdom. Now there is a great kingdom set up on earth, consisting of all God's people, and its ruler is Christ. As such, His duties are here said to be three fold. 1. He makes us willing to obey Him. 2. He gives us laws for our guidance and safety. 3. He limits and finally puts down all who oppose us and Him.[2]

Out of the Mouths of Babes

So when the children of Jerusalem uttered the words 'Hosanna to the Son of David' to the Lord Jesus, they were affirming a profound truth about both the person and work of Christ. Their words revealed Jesus as the Saviour of sinners, coequal with God. And their words revealed that they recognised Him as the longed-for Messiah, who would bring in God's promised kingdom of blessedness. Jesus commended them. To their opponents and detractors He employed the words of the Psalmist that have become an everyday expression: 'Jesus said to them, "… Have you never read, 'Out of the mouth of babes and nursing infants You have perfected praise'?"' (Matt. 21:16).

---

1. From the *Westminster Shorter Catechism*, the answer to Question 26.
2. *Shorter Catechism with commentary and Scripture Proofs*, Rev Roderick Lawson, The Sabbath School Society for Ireland (n.d.), p. 21

Out of the mouths of babes

Children of Jerusalem
Sang the praise of Jesus' name:
Children, too, of modern days
Join to sing the Savior's praise.

Parents, teachers, old and young,
All unite to swell the song;
Higher and yet higher rise,
'Til hosannas fill the skies.

Hark, hark, hark! While infant voices sing,
Hark, hark, hark! While infant voices sing,
Loud hosannas, loud hosannas,
Loud hosannas to our King.

(John Henley, 1800–42)

19

Philistine!

To call someone a 'Philistine' is to view such a person in a derogatory way. Popularly used, the term 'Philistine' is meant as a reference to an uncultured person—one who does not appreciate the supposed finer matters in life—things such as classical music, great art or the theatre. When a tight rein has to be kept on public spending due to financial constraints, and subsidising the arts is not seen as a government priority, accusations of being 'Philistines' are sometimes thrown at the government.

The original name 'Philistine' refers to a people who lived in Philistia, an area south-west of the Promised Land of Israel. Their land was dominated by five cities, each ruled by a 'lord'. From the time of the Judges—Shamgar and notably Samson were Judges who both battled against the Philistines—until they were subdued under the reign of David, the Philistines were a constant thorn in the side of the people of Israel. Being near neighbours, they had designs on the land of Israel and used to invade the land, causing havoc and misery. The Philistines' expertise in metalworking was highly advantageous to them in military terms. Perhaps the most famous Philistine was the warrior, Goliath. He truly was a giant of a man, measuring some ten feet in height. The Bible describes his metallic, defensive armour and offensive weapons in impressive detail. Young David's unlikely defeat of Goliath 'in the name of the LORD of hosts, the God of the armies of Israel' (1 Sam. 17:45) is one of the famous incidents in Old Testament history.

The Philistines had their own religion and their own gods. Their chief god was Dagon, but they also worshipped the gods of Beelzebub and Ashtoreth. They worshipped these, believing that they were responsible for their agricultural welfare and fertility. During a low point in Israel's history, when Israel battled against the Philistines, the Philistines captured the ark of God. The ark of God was the sacred box which contained the tables of the law. It symbolised the presence of God with His people. The problem was that while Israel had the ark of the Lord, the Lord of the ark had withdrawn His blessing from them because of the Israelites' disobedience. The ark itself had, in a very real sense, replaced the Lord. The physical had overtaken the spiritual. Faith in the Lord Himself had been replaced by the equivalent of a lucky charm. The Bible states that 'Then the Philistines took the ark of God and brought it from Ebenezer to Ashdod. When the Philistines took the ark of God, they brought it into the house of Dagon and set it by Dagon' (1 Sam. 5:1,2).

This military victory over Israel, along with the capturing of the ark of God suggested, seemingly quite logically, that the Philistines were militarily superior to Israel, and that their gods were greater than theirs. But this was not so. What followed can only be explained miraculously. It can only be understood as an intervention of the one, true God. The God of Israel intervened to show that He alone is the one, true God, superior to all, and that all must bow down to Him:

> And when the people of Ashdod arose early in the morning, there was Dagon, fallen on its face to the earth before the ark of the LORD. So they took Dagon and set it in its place again. And when they arose early the next morning, there was Dagon, fallen on its face to the ground before the ark

of the LORD. The head of Dagon and both the palms of its hands *were* broken off on the threshold; only Dagon's *torso* was left of it. Therefore neither the priests of Dagon nor any who come into Dagon's house tread on the threshold of Dagon in Ashdod to this day (1 Sam. 5:3-5).

So much for Dagon! Events followed quickly. God next sent a terrible plague on the Philistines. All the males broke out in tumours. They hurriedly sent the ark of the Lord back to the land of Israel, along with a guilt-offering with a view to staying the hand of the Lord which was against them. The event had a sobering effect on the Philistines—and it also had a sobering effect on the people of Israel, causing them to return to the Lord in repentance. Sometime later we read:

Then Samuel spoke to all the house of Israel, saying, 'If you return to the Lord with all your hearts, *then* put away the foreign gods and the Ashtoreths from among you, and prepare your hearts for the LORD, and serve Him only; and He will deliver you from the hand of the Philistines.' So the children of Israel put away the Baals and the Ashtoreths, and served the LORD only (1 Sam. 7:3-4).

What about the Philistines? They were employed by God as an instrument to chastise His people when they had strayed from Him. 'For whom the LORD loves He chastens, and scourges every son whom He receives' (Heb. 12:6). The Philistines worshipped false gods—idols. The Bible states that idolatry is a heinous sin, for in the first and foremost commandment, God states that 'You shall have no other gods before Me' (Exod. 20:3). The God of Israel—the God of the Bible, who created and sustains the universe—is the only God there is. He is infinitely superior and supreme over all. He has no rivals and He tolerates no rivals. He alone can affirm, 'For I *am* God, and *there* is no other; I *am* God, and *there is* none like Me' (Isa. 46:9).

The temptation of idolatry never goes away. Christians today are not immune from the temptation of worshipping at the shrines of the false gods of money, worldly success, human fame and the celebrity culture, etc. Idolatry is as pointless as it is sinful, for idols are powerless to bring eternal salvation or earthly satisfaction. Jesus reminds us that 'this is eternal life, that they may know You, the only true God, and Jesus Christ whom You have sent' (John 17:3). And the apostle Paul similarly gives us the warning: 'For even if there are so-called gods, whether in heaven or on earth (as there are many gods and many lords), yet for us *there* is one God, the Father, of whom *are* all things, and we for Him; and one Lord Jesus Christ, through whom *are* all things, and through whom we *live*' (1 Cor. 8:5-6).

20

Pour out your heart

'He poured out his heart to me.' Any Christian pastor with a true heart for ministry will know the meaning of this expression. While pastors should be known for their gift of speech in the pulpit on a Sunday—where they explain and apply the Word of God—careful listening skills are a requirement of their pastoral visitation during the week. An old advertising slogan for a telecommunication company told people that 'It is good to talk.' Another saying makes the point that 'a problem shared is a problem halved.' Pastors are to have listening ears. James 1:19 applies especially to pastoral visitation: 'Let every man be swift to hear, slow to speak, slow to wrath.' Those under a pastor's care must feel that he is approachable and trustworthy and that, if needs be, they can meet him in private, and 'pour out their heart' to him, assured of his confidentiality, sympathy and prayerful concern.

The expression 'to pour out your heart' originates from the Bible. In Psalm 62:8 we read the injunction 'Trust in Him at all times, you people; pour out your heart before Him; God *is* a refuge for us.' Similarly, in Lamentations 2:19 we read, 'Pour out your heart like water before the face of the Lord.'

While having the ear of a sympathetic friend or pastor at a time of need is a blessing not to be despised, every Christian has an even greater blessing. Christians are privileged to have the ear of none less than Almighty God Himself. Through Christ we may approach Him. In prayer we may actually talk to the Master of the universe Himself. By His grace to us in Christ, we may even address Him as 'Abba, Father', assured of His love, wisdom, sympathy and concern, and His superabundant ability

91

to meet our needs in answer to our prayers. Psalm 55:22 encourages us to 'Cast your burden on the LORD, and He shall sustain you.' Peter surely had this verse in mind when he guided his readers to be 'casting all your care upon Him, for He cares for you' (1 Pet. 5:7). The burdens of this life may well lie heavily upon us. The Bible, however, enjoins us to unburden our burdens on God Himself. The omnipotent Creator and Sustainer of the universe is well able to bear them. He Who is infinite in wisdom and power is able to handle our burdens far better than we can!

Encouragements to pray run right through the Bible. It has been well said that prayer is not a matter of overcoming God's reluctance, but rather taking hold of God's willingness. Philippians 4:6 states that we are to 'Be anxious for nothing, but in everything by prayer and supplication, with thanksgiving, let your requests be made known to God.' Hebrews 4:16 calls us to confidence in the merits and mediation of Christ in these words: 'Let us therefore come boldly to the throne of grace, that we may obtain mercy and find grace to help in time of need.' And in Psalm 50:15, God Himself speaks and says, 'Call upon Me in the day of trouble; I will deliver you, and you shall glorify Me.' John Calvin comments on this verse:

This last passage points out that there are two sorts of prayer: invocation (or request) and thanksgiving. In request we set out before God what our hearts desire. In thanksgiving we acknowledge the blessings he has given us. And we must make sure that we constantly use both kinds of prayer. This is because we are plagued with such poverty and destitution that even the best of us must sigh and groan continually, and call on the Lord with all humility. On the other hand, the generous gifts which the Lord lavishes upon us in his goodness are so very abundant that, wherever we look, the wonders of his works are seen to be so great, that we always have reason for praise and thanksgiving.[1]

So we return to our verse: 'Pour out your heart before Him' (Ps. 62:8). What a privilege so to do! In private before God, there can be no pretence—nor need there be. When we pray in private, our public masks are taken off. To quote Calvin again, 'Prayer has not been instituted that we might arrogantly exalt ourselves before God, nor that we should extol our dignity, but so that we might admit our poverty, groaning like children, telling their father about their troubles.'[2] The well-known hymn on prayer puts it so well:

> What a friend we have in Jesus,
> All our sins and griefs to bear!
> What a privilege to carry
> Everything to God in prayer!
> Oh, what peace we often forfeit,
> Oh, what needless pain we bear,
> All because we do not carry
> Everything to God in prayer!
>
> Have we trials and temptations?
> Is there trouble anywhere?
> We should never be discouraged—
> Take it to the Lord in prayer.
> Can we find a friend so faithful,
> Who will all our sorrows share?

---

1. *Truth for all Time,* p. 53
2. Ibid, p. 52

A Pinch of Salt

Jesus knows our every weakness;
Take it to the Lord in prayer.

Are we weak and heavy-laden,
Cumbered with a load of care?
Precious Saviour, still our refuge—
Take it to the Lord in prayer.
Do thy friends despise, forsake thee?
Take it to the Lord in prayer!
In His arms He'll take and shield thee,
Thou wilt find a solace there.

(Joseph Scriven, 1819-86)

21

Practise what you preach

An apocryphal tale tells of a minister's wife entering his study with a cup of coffee for him, not long before he was due to leave for church. She noticed that he was looking over his sermon notes for the impending church service. 'Ah, practising what you preach, are you dear?' she remarked.

The expression 'to practise what you preach' is usually used negatively and scornfully. It refers to saying one thing and yet doing another. For example, here is a doctor out to promote good health—yet he himself is spotted smoking and drinking. And here is a dentist who is unable to give up sugar in his tea. Then, sadly, scandals in the church are not unknown. And here is a Member of Parliament who espouses equality for all. It transpires, however, that he sends his children to a public school, not to a state school. When hypocrisy is uncovered, the expression is used: 'You should practise what you preach.'

Did you know that the Lord Jesus Christ used the expression 'practise what you preach'? In Matthew 23:1-3 we read: 'Then Jesus spoke to the multitudes and to His disciples, saying: "The scribes and the Pharisees sit in Moses' seat. Therefore whatever they tell you to observe, *that* observe and do, but do not do according to their works; for they say, and do not do."'

The Lord Jesus—in His particular words—and the Bible in general are vehemently opposed to religious hypocrisy. The emphasis of the Bible is on a real, personal, inward relationship with God Himself as well as on the reality of this relationship being seen in us day by day. *Positively*, the message of the Old

Testament prophets is summarised in Micah 6:8: 'He has shown you, O man, what *is* good; and what does the LORD require of you but to do justly, to love mercy, and to walk humbly with your God?' *Negatively*, however, Isaiah, who lived at the same time as Micah, denounced those whose religion was a mere lip service—those whose lives and lips went in opposite directions. God, through Isaiah, spoke, and complained, 'Inasmuch as these people draw near with their mouths and honor Me with their lips, but have removed their hearts far from Me, and their fear toward Me is taught by the commandment of men' (Isa. 29:13).

Christians, then, are to practise what they preach—that is, to live out the Christian life. James, in his epistle of applied Christianity wrote, 'But be doers of the word, and not hearers only, deceiving yourselves' (James 1:22). So, if I claim to know that God in Christ at Calvary has forgiven all my sins, it is hypocritical of me to bear grudges against others. If I claim to belong to Jesus and know something of His love, then something of the love of Christ *has* to be manifested in my life. If I claim to know that God is my Father, it is hypocritical of me to be wracked by worry. It suggests He is incapable or unwilling to care for His children and that His providence cannot be trusted. And if I claim to have been saved by the grace of God in Christ, I will vote with my feet on Sundays, and be found in a congregation of God's people, gathered to worship Him and hear His Word.

Yes, we are saved by faith alone in Christ alone. But faith works. James, once again, denounced dead, nominal faith, and stated that 'faith by itself, if it does not have works, is dead' (James 2:17). He was suggesting that just as a healthy tree bears good fruit, so it is also in the Christian life, and that a genuine believer, even if not sinless, will bear good spiritual fruit to the glory of God. Such is the fruit of a Christlike character, the fruit of faithfulness to the tasks which God has assigned, the fruit of a desire to share the good news of the Lord Jesus Christ. The Christian faith is not a spectator sport! Remember James' words: 'Be doers of the word, and not hearers only' (James 1:22).

The godly Bishop J. C. Ryle once wrote these words:

> The Lord Jesus bids you 'occupy'. By that He means that you are to be a 'doer' in your Christianity, and not merely a hearer and professor. He wants His servants not only to receive His wages and eat His bread and dwell in His house and belong to His family, but also to do His work. You are to 'let your light so shine before men that they may see your good works.' Have you faith? It must not be a dead faith; it must 'work by love'. Are you elect? You are elect unto 'obedience'. Are you redeemed? You are redeemed that you may be 'a peculiar people, zealous of good works'. Do you love Christ? Prove the reality of your love by keeping Christ's commandments. Oh reader, do not forget this charge to 'Occupy'.[1]

So may God give us grace to be real Christians, and to know what it is to work out what He has worked in us! May God deliver us from ever bringing reproach to the name and cause of Christ. May God give us grace to know, love, serve and obey Him better. May God give us grace to 'Practise what we preach'.

---

1. J.C. Ryle, *Occupy Until I Come!*, from Coming Events and Present Duties—Being Plain Papers on Prophecy, 1879, from http://gracegems. org/Ryle/coming_events_and_present_duties3.htm, accessed March 22nd, 2014.

22

Pride goes before a fall

'Pride goes before a fall.' I first heard this proverb when I was in primary school—along with such sayings as 'A stitch in time saves nine' and 'Too many cooks spoil the broth.'

'Pride goes before a fall.' Unknown to me and my primary school classmates, this saying actually comes from the Bible. The reference is Proverbs 16:18 and the verse reads, 'Pride *goes* before destruction, and a haughty spirit before a fall.' Hebrew poetry often employs a device known as synonymous parallelism where the second line repeats the thought of the first line, but using different words. This is the case here as 'pride' and 'a haughty spirit' are synonyms—as are 'destruction' and 'a fall'. Our saying thus originates in Proverbs 16:18, but the same sentiment is found elsewhere in the book of Proverbs. Proverbs 18:12 similarly reads, 'Before destruction the heart of a man is haughty, and before honor *is* humility.' And Proverbs 11:2 states: 'When pride comes, then comes shame; but with the humble *is* wisdom.' Then when we turn to the New Testament, we glean that the Lord Jesus Himself taught, 'For whoever exalts himself will be humbled, and he who humbles himself will be exalted' (Luke 14:11), and both James and Peter warned that God opposes the proud but gives grace to the humble (see James 4:6; 1 Pet. 5:5).

Pride Goes Before Destruction: An Example

The Bible teaches by example as well as by precept. It was pride that preceded King Nebuchadnezzar's fall in Old Testament times, during Daniel's exile in Babylon. Daniel records:

At the end of the twelve months he was walking about the royal palace of Babylon. The king spoke, saying, 'Is not this great Babylon, that I have built for a royal dwelling by my mighty power and for the honor of my majesty?'

While the word *was still* in the king's mouth, a voice fell from heaven: 'King Nebuchadnezzar, to you it is spoken: the kingdom has departed from you! And they shall drive you from men, and your dwelling *shall be* with the beasts of the field' (Dan. 4:29-32).

And God's decree was immediately fulfilled. Nebuchadnezzar was humiliated. 'That very hour the word was fulfilled concerning Nebuchadnezzar; he was driven from men and ate grass like oxen; his body was wet with the dew of heaven till his hair had grown like eagles' *feathers* and his nails like birds' *claws*' (Dan. 4:33). The blessing, however, was that Nebuchadnezzar eventually returned to his senses from his madness, and turned to the one true God in repentance and humility. He made the telling confession, 'Now I, Nebuchadnezzar, praise and extol and honor the King of heaven, all of whose works *are* truth, and His ways justice. And those who walk in pride He is able to put down' (v. 37).

Then, when we consider the New Testament, we read of another king—one of the Herod dynasty—whose pride led to his downfall. Herod reigned in Caesarea on the coast. One day he sat proudly in his royal robes before the people and made a speech before them. Luke records how 'the people kept shouting, "The voice of a god and not of a man!" Then immediately an angel of the Lord struck him, because he did not give glory to God. And he was eaten by worms and died' (Acts 12:22-23).

Pride Goes Before Destruction: An Explanation

The question is this: Why is pride condemned so strongly in the Bible? The answer is that pride dethrones God and puts self on the throne. Sinful pride is practical atheism. Sinful pride's self-sufficiency and self-congratulation is a denial of our total dependence on God and His grace.

Pride can cast us into eternal hell, for pride can suggest that 'I am the master of my fate and captain of my soul.' Pride can suggest that we are acceptable to God by what we are and by what we do—as if we could put Almighty God into our debt. It is the role of the Holy Spirit, however, to convince us of our personal inadequacy and unfitness for God's presence—that we are actually sinners under His wrath, and eternally lost apart from the grace of God in Christ.

The gospel, however, proclaims that the righteousness which we lack may be obtained. It is not obtained or attained by ourselves, though. It is not a self-righteousness, but the righteousness of Christ, freely given to us and received by humble faith—'not having my own righteousness, which *is* from the law, but that which *is* through faith in Christ, the righteousness which is from God by faith' (Phil. 3:9). The Lord Jesus taught this in His well-known parable of the Pharisee and the tax collector. Here, the Pharisee proudly extolled his own supposed self-righteousness before God. The tax collector, however, cast himself solely on God's mercy, confessing that he was a sinner and as such had no righteousness to plead his case before God. Jesus concluded: 'I tell you, this man [the tax collector] went down to his house justified rather than the other; for everyone who exalts himself will be humbled, and he who humbles himself will be exalted' (Luke 18:14).

Pride therefore is a false—and a damnable—confidence in ourselves, blinding us to our need of God's mercy. Pride suggests that we are not in need of the redeeming work of Christ and that the cross was therefore unnecessary.

Pride: An Insidious Sin

Christians however—those saved by God's grace in Christ—are also not immune from the danger of pride, as no Christian is immune from temptation. The danger is especially acute when all seems to be going well for us and during times of ease and prosperity. It is during such times that we can forget that it is in God that 'we live and move and have our being' (Acts 17:28) and that we are totally dependent on His providence for all things. Hence, in Old Testament times, before Israel entered the Promised Land, God warned:

> Beware that you do not forget the LORD your God... lest—*when* you have eaten and are full, and have built beautiful houses and dwell *in them*; and *when* your herds and your flocks multiply, and your silver and your gold are multiplied, and all that you have is multiplied; when your heart is lifted up, and you forget the LORD your God who brought you out of the land of Egypt, from the house of bondage (Deut. 8:11-14).

According to the Bible, there is no such thing as 'a self-made man'. All our abilities—latent and developed—are God-given. 'And what do you have that you did not receive? Now if you did indeed receive *it*, why do you boast as if you had not received *it*?' (1 Cor. 4:7). And so the Bible warns you to guard your heart in this regard: 'You say in your heart, "My power and the might of my hand have gained me this wealth." And you shall remember the

LORD your God, for *it is* He who gives you power to get wealth...'
(see Deut. 8:17,18).

Blessing from Buffeting

The heading above may give us an insight into the trials and
difficulties of life—why God sends us trials and difficulties
is a mystery—but the trials of life knock away our pride and
self-sufficiency, and remind us of our frailty and our total
dependence on God. If trials and tribulations, pain and
perplexity, and losses and crosses draw us closer to God and
cause us to cast ourselves on Him alone for help and support,
surely they are blessings in disguise, for God alone is the fount
of every blessing. This, at any rate, was the way the apostle
Paul viewed trials. He related how once 'we were burdened
beyond measure, above strength, so that we despaired even
of life. Yes, we had the sentence of death in ourselves, that we
should not trust in ourselves but in God who raises the dead'
(2 Cor. 1:8,9). God promised Paul—and God promises us—
that in our earthly trials 'My grace is sufficient for you, for My
strength is made perfect in weakness' (2 Cor. 12:9). How many
times has our extremity proved to be God's opportunity? How
many times has our inadequacy caused us to prove God's total
adequacy? His grace is surely sufficient for us!

So beware of pride, for the proverb states: 'Pride *goes* before
destruction, and a haughty spirit before a fall.' (Prov. 16:18). We
will let Almighty God have the closing word. Through His servant
Jeremiah, He still exhorts us:

'Let not the wise *man* glory in his wisdom,
Let not the mighty *man* glory in his might,
Nor let the rich *man* glory in his riches;

But let him who glories glory in this,
That he understands and knows Me,
That I *am* the LORD, exercising lovingkindness, judgment,
and righteousness in the earth.
For in these I delight,' says the LORD (Jer. 9:23-24).

23

Please don't put words into my mouth

We sometimes hear two opposite expressions. One goes, 'You took the words right out of my mouth.' The expression is used when someone thinks the same thought as we're thinking and articulates it just before we were about to do so. The other expression goes, 'Please don't put words into my mouth.' This expression is used when someone accuses us of saying something we did not say. Perhaps that person has put a 'spin' on what we said, distorting what we meant. Or perhaps there has been complete misunderstanding of the words we spoke, and it has worked out to be a case of 'getting the wrong end of the stick'.

The expression 'to put words into my mouth' goes back a long way. It goes back to the time of Moses in about 1300 B.C. The book of Exodus reveals that Almighty God Himself was the first Person to 'put words into the mouth' of someone else.

Exodus 3 and 4 record how God called Moses to lead the people of Israel out of slavery in Egypt and into the Promised Land. To begin with, Moses was overawed. He did not feel competent for the task, and had doubts over his leadership ability. So he protested to God that the people of Israel might not 'believe me or listen to my voice' (Exod. 4:1). The Scripture then continues:

> Then Moses said to the LORD, 'O my Lord, I *am* not eloquent, neither before nor since You have spoken to Your servant; but I *am* slow of speech and slow of tongue.'

105

So the LORD said to him, 'Who has made man's mouth? Or who makes the mute, the deaf, the seeing, or the blind? *Have* not I, the LORD? Now therefore, go, and I will be with your mouth and teach you what you shall say' (Exod. 4:10-12).

Almighty God therefore promised Moses that He would 'be with your [his] mouth' and so give him the gift of eloquence and fluent speech. Sad to say, Moses continued to protest. He shrank from the public speaking role God had assigned him and wished to delegate it. God then relented and allowed Aaron, Moses' brother, to do the speaking on Moses' behalf. God thus explained to Moses:

Now you shall speak to him and put the words in his mouth. And I will be with your mouth and with his mouth, and I will teach you what you shall do. So he shall be your spokesman to the people. And he himself shall be as a mouth for you, and you shall be to him as God (Exod. 4:15-16).

The Nature of Prophecy
Moses' obituary stated that 'there has [had] not arisen in Israel a prophet like Moses, whom the LORD knew face to face' (Deut. 34:10). Moses is revealed in the Bible as being the archetypal prophet. God's actual giving to him of the words that He wished to speak—putting words into his mouth—reveals to us the true nature of biblical prophecy and the true nature of the Bible—the written Word of God itself.

In the Bible, the prophets were God's spokesmen. As such, they were both forth tellers and foretellers—speakers and seers. They were called to deliver God's words unadulterated by any mixture of human words—even though, in a mysterious way, God did not bypass their individual personalities. The prophets were channels of the Word of God. Theirs was a 'Thus says the LORD' ministry. The Spirit of God revealed to them the exact message and words God intended His people to know. As Peter put it: 'Prophecy never came by the will of man, but holy men of God spoke *as they were* moved by the Holy Spirit' (2 Pet. 1:21).

The Nature of the Bible

What was true of biblical prophecy—the spoken Word of God through the prophets—is equally true of the written Word of God which we have today—the Holy Bible. While there are many human authors of the Bible, the ultimate Author is God Himself for 'All Scripture *is* given by inspiration of God ...' (2 Tim. 3:16), that is 'All Scripture is God-breathed' (NIV). The divine inspiration of the Scriptures is a fundamental of the Christian faith. The divine inspiration of the Scriptures explains why the Bible is the Book of God. The inerrancy of Scripture is a consequence of divine inspiration. What do we mean when we refer here to 'divine inspiration'? Divine inspiration refers to the supernatural operation and influence of the Holy Spirit of God on the authors of Scripture so that they wrote exactly what God wanted them to write. They wrote what God wanted us to know. They wrote the very Word of God—nothing more, nothing less, nothing else:

> How precious is the Book Divine,
> By inspiration given!
> Bright as a lamp its doctrines shine
> To guide our souls to heaven.
>
> Its light, descending from above
> Our gloomy world to cheer,

Displays a Savior's boundless love
And brings his glories near.

(John Fawcett, 1782)

This leads us to consider the centre of the centre of Scripture, who is none other than the Lord Jesus Christ.

The Incarnate Word

The prophets spoke the Word of God. In doing so, they revealed the mind of God. Words are the verbal articulation of the thoughts of our mind. The staggering message of the Bible, however, is that in Christ, the Word of God actually took on our human form and visited our planet. 'And the Word became flesh and dwelt among us, and we beheld His glory, the glory as of the only begotten of the Father, full of grace and truth' (John 1:14). Jesus spoke the words of God, for sure. He said, 'The Father who sent Me gave Me a command, what I should say and what I should speak.' (John 12:49). Yet Jesus is more than just a speaker of God's Words. He is the very Word of God incarnate. As such He is the unsurpassed and unsurpassable revelation of the one true God. 'For in Him dwells all the fullness of the Godhead bodily' (Col. 2:9). He could thus say, 'He who has seen Me has seen the Father' (John 14:9).

It is in the Bible that we encounter Jesus. The inspired Word and the incarnate Word are distinguishable, yet intermesh in our experience. Moses was the archetypal prophet. God put words into his mouth. Yet Jesus—the Saviour of sinners—is the ultimate Prophet. He is the Word of God in the flesh. He is the subject of prophecy and He is the fulfilment and culmination of prophecy. He reveals to us the will of God for our salvation. To summarise:

You put the words into my mouth

'God, who at various times and in various ways spoke in time past to the fathers by the prophets, has in these last days spoken to us by *His* Son' (Heb. 1:1-2).

Great Prophet of my God,
My tongue shall bless thy name;
By thee the joyful news
Of our salvation came:
The joyful news of sins forgiven,
Of hell subdued, and peace with heaven.

(Isaac Watts, 1674–1748)

24

Root and branch

We use the expression 'root and branch' to denote thoroughness or completeness. For example, a football manager is sacked and a new one is appointed in his place. As soon as he has settled in, he makes changes right across the board—he replaces the coaching staff, he sells some players and buys others, and he changes the team's whole ethos and style of play. When this occurs, the newspapers might report that 'On the new manager's appointment, changes were made root and branch.'

Few realise that the expression 'root and branch' is a biblical one. It originates in the last chapter of the last book of the Old Testament—the prophecy of Malachi. Under the inspiration of the Holy Spirit, Malachi was able to speak for God, and foretold the coming, final judgement day. And so in Malachi 4:1 we read: '"For behold, the day is coming, burning like an oven, and all the proud, yes, all who do wickedly will be stubble. And the day which is coming shall burn them up," says the LORD of hosts, "that will leave them neither *root nor branch.*"'

The final judgement of the impenitent wicked, therefore, will be a judgement that is 'root and branch'. Almighty God's work will be absolutely thorough. No crimes will be left unpunished, no sins will be left un-condemned, and all wrongs will be put right for eternity. In this life it is not unknown for criminals to 'get away with it'. A notorious example in the U.K. is that of the late celebrity Jimmy Savile. Since his death in 2011 it has transpired that he was a lifelong abuser of children. During his life he was never once prosecuted for this. In fact, he enjoyed a millionaire lifestyle beyond the reach of most people. Savile escaped justice in this life—but he will not escape divine judgement in the next. God will see to it, promising that 'all who do wickedly will be stubble. And the day which is coming shall burn them up… that will leave them neither *root nor branch.*'

The eternal lot of the wicked, therefore, is in infinite contrast with the eternal lot of God's people—those who have been granted the gift of repentance and saving faith by God. While the lot of the wicked will be eternal punishment, the lot of the righteous will be eternal joy. Malachi's very next verse—after his 'root and branch' verse—tells us, 'But to you who fear My name the Sun of Righteousness shall arise with healing in His wings; and you shall go out and grow fat like stall-fed calves' (Mal. 4:2). This is a reference to the coming Messiah—the Lord Jesus Christ—and the liberation He brings. Christ is the Christian's righteousness. And He is the One who brings healing—He is the One who heals our broken relationship with God, caused by our sin.

> Jesus, Thy blood and righteousness
> My beauty are, my glorious dress;
> Midst flaming worlds, in these arrayed,
> With joy shall I lift up my head.

(Nicolaus L von Zinzendorf, 1700–60)

The prospect of God's 'root and branch' coming judgement is, paradoxically, both a comforting one and an unsettling one. It is comforting, because it is good to know that justice will be done and that God will right all the wrongs that frustrate and anger us in the current era. The Bible tells us that the impenitent wicked—those who have rebelled against God, blatantly flouted His law and brought misery to their fellow men—will spend eternity in the flames of hell. 'But the cowardly, unbelieving, abominable, murderers, sexually immoral, sorcerers, idolaters, and all liars shall have their part in the lake which burns with fire and brimstone, which is the second death' (Rev. 21:8).

The Bad News of Judgement

The prospect of God's 'root and branch' judgement, however, is also very unsettling, as we know within ourselves that we have not truly loved and obeyed Him with all our hearts. While we may not be guilty before an earthly court, we will certainly be declared guilty if we are tried before God's heavenly one, for God's law is concerned with inward attitudes as well as outward actions. God will punish lustful thoughts as well as adultery and fornication. God will punish covetousness as well as stealing. God will punish hatred as well as murder. Breaking God's law just once—in spirit as well as in action—is enough to render us liable to eternal punishment. Sinning against an eternal God has eternal consequences. James wrote, 'For whoever shall keep the whole law, and yet stumble in one *point*, he is guilty of all' (James 2:10).

The Good News of Justification

But there is hope for us, as there is a gospel of saving grace. Sinners can be saved because 'Christ Jesus came into the world to save sinners' (1 Tim. 1:15). Christians have the assurance that 'God did not appoint us to wrath, but to obtain salvation through our Lord Jesus Christ' (1 Thess. 5:9). It is Jesus' death on the cross which saves sinners. At Calvary, He was punished for our sins so that we might be pardoned for our sins. His was truly a 'root and branch' punishment by God that we might know— through union with Him—a 'root and branch' pardon from God.

Christians rejoice in the finished work of Calvary. While God's law condemns us, Christ the Lord has redeemed us. On the cross, in our place, He incurred the penalty for our breaking of God's law. He was judged so that we might be justified. He was treated as guilty so that we might be declared not guilty. He was cursed so that we might be eternally blessed. 'Christ has redeemed us from the curse of the law, having become a curse for us (for it is written, "Cursed is everyone who hangs on a tree")' (Gal. 3:13).

So it is the Lord Jesus Christ—foretold by Malachi as 'the Sun of Righteousness'—who makes the difference between judgement and mercy, heaven and hell, eternal life and eternal loss. He is the Saviour of sinners. God is just. He cannot violate His own law—hence the 'root and branch' judgement that is pending. But the gospel proclaims that '*there is* therefore now no condemnation to those who are in Christ Jesus' (Rom. 8:1). In the mercy of God, Jesus stepped in and was judged in our place to save us from judgement. The little poem expresses this so succinctly:

> He knew how wicked man had been,
> And knew that God must punish sin;
> So out of pity, Jesus said,
> He'd bear the punishment instead.

> (James Robert Brown, 1828)

Christians are eternal debtors to God's mercy:

> A debtor to mercy alone,
> Of covenant mercy I sing;
> Nor fear, with Thy righteousness on;
> My person and off'ring to bring.

Root and branch

The terrors of law and of God
With me can have nothing to do;
My Saviour's obedience and blood
Hide all my transgressions from view.

(Augustus Montague Toplady, 1740–88)

25

Shake off the dust from your feet

'You should shake off the dust from your feet.' We sometimes hear this expression in the context of an act of repudiation and severance. It can be used against either an individual or an institution, when we want nothing more to do with such. For example, we have had trouble resolving a bill with Utility Firm A. The customer service they give us proves frustrating and unsatisfactory. We thus change to Utility Firm B. Symbolically, we 'shake off the dust from our feet' concerning Utility Firm A.

The expression concerning shaking off the dust from our feet was well known in the time of the Lord Jesus, and taken up by Him and the apostles in their ministry. The Pharisees, it is believed, literally used to shake off the dust from their footwear after they had visited a Gentile area. Such a physical act—as with the ritual hand-washing—was symbolic of the desire to avoid spiritual contamination from 'unclean Gentiles'.

Matthew 10:5 and the following verses relate the Lord Jesus sending out His disciples on the first ever gospel mission. They were to proclaim by both word and action that in Christ, the kingdom of heaven had arrived, and that sinners should respond to this with repentance and faith. The reception given to the disciples—as in gospel ministry today—would no doubt be mixed, Jesus foretold. Some would respond positively and welcome the disciples. Others, no doubt would be apathetic. And yet others would respond negatively with hostility. Jesus said of the latter: 'And whoever will not receive you nor hear your words, when you depart from that house or city, *shake off the dust from your feet.* Assuredly, I say to you, it will be more tolerable for the land of Sodom and Gomorrah in the day of judgment than for that city!' (Matt. 10:14,15).

Shaking off the dust from the feet in such an instance was a very solemn act—an act of warning to those who rejected the gospel of salvation. Compare Jesus' words in Luke 9:5: 'And whoever will not receive you, when you go out of that city, *shake off the very dust from your feet as a testimony against them.*'

When the apostle Paul and his missionary companions visited Antioch in Pisidia, they proclaimed the good news of Jesus, as they normally did—that 'through this Man is preached to you the forgiveness of sins' (Acts 13:38). Paul certainly caused a stir, for, as Luke tells us, 'On the next Sabbath almost the whole city came together to hear the word of God' (Acts 13:44). As was often the case, however, the response to Paul's preaching was polarised. On the one hand, 'as many as had been appointed to eternal life believed' (Acts 13:48). But on the other hand, 'the Jews stirred up the devout and prominent women and the chief men of the city, raised up persecution against Paul and Barnabas, and expelled them from their region' (Acts 13:50). And what was Paul's and Barnabas' response? They '*shook off the dust from their feet against them*' (Acts 13:51). It was an act testifying against them for their unbelief. It was an act of separation—as if to say, 'We wish no part in their unbelief.' It was also an act of exoneration: 'We have told you the way of salvation. We cannot be held responsible if you bring condemnation on yourself.' Compare Paul's testimony to some unbelieving Jews in Corinth: 'But when they opposed him and blasphemed, he shook *his* garments and said to them, "Your blood *be* upon your *own* heads; I am clean. From now on I will go to the Gentiles"' (Acts 18:6).

'Shake off the dust from your feet.' What do we learn from this expression as it is used in the Bible? The main lesson is that of our individual or personal, human responsibility to believe in Jesus while we may, as another opportunity may not arise, and so we will bring eternal condemnation on ourselves. As a Christian who embraces the Reformed faith, I delight in the doctrine of divine sovereignty. The absolute control of Almighty God over all things is the ultimate comfort for the human soul. Yet the Bible also, paradoxically perhaps, teaches that God will hold human beings individually accountable for their actions. On the day of judgement we will not be able to plead divine election— God's eternal choice of some to be saved and His bypassing of others—as an excuse for our unbelief.

The Bible teaches that God is longsuffering—'not willing that any should perish but that all should come to repentance' (2 Pet. 3:9). Yet no one should presume on this divine forbearance, for the Bible also teaches us that Almighty God gives some people over to their unbelief. It is as if He, after repeated warnings, complies with their wishes, leaving them to live and die with the eternal consequences of their wish to decline His offer of grace. 'He who is often rebuked, *and* hardens *his* neck, will suddenly be destroyed, and that without remedy' (Prov. 29:1).

In Genesis 6:3 we read that 'the LORD said, "My Spirit shall not strive with man forever..."' a text suggesting that there is a fixed period to define the day of grace, beyond which there is no hope of salvation. When an individual rejects the pangs of conscience and the pleadings of the gospel message, and scorns both the message and the messenger, the messenger is free from responsibility if he has faithfully proclaimed Christ as the only Saviour. 'Yet, if you warn the wicked, and he does not turn from his wickedness, nor from his wicked way, he shall die in his iniquity; but you have delivered your soul' (Ezek. 3:19). There is thus a serious and solemn side to gospel ministry, dealing with the matters of eternity as it does. Jesus said to His disciples, 'He who hears you hears Me, he who rejects you rejects Me, and he who rejects Me rejects Him who sent Me' (Luke 10:16). The Bible exhortation is to 'believe on the Lord Jesus Christ, and you will be saved' (Acts 16:31). We are not to tempt the patience of God, for 'Behold, now *is* the accepted time; behold, now *is* the day of salvation' (2 Cor. 6:2).

Life at best is very brief,
Like the falling of a leaf,
Like the binding of a sheaf,
Be in time!
Fleeting days are telling fast
That the die will soon be cast,
And the fatal line be passed,
Be in time!

Fairest flowers soon decay,
Youth and beauty pass away;
O you have not long to stay,
Be in time!
While God's Spirit bids you come,
Sinner do no longer roam,
Lest you seal your hopeless doom,
Be in time!

Be in time! Be in time!
While the voice of Jesus calls you,
Be in time!
If in sin you longer wait,
You may find no open gate,
And your cry be just too late:
Be in time!

(Charles Harrison Mason, 1866–1961)

26

Sour grapes

'Sour grapes.' This phrase refers to a pretended disdain for something we secretly desire but cannot have—the disparagement of something we would like, but which is beyond our reach. If you can't have it, put it down and say that it isn't all that it is made out to be!

Here is a fictitious example of 'sour grapes'. I would dearly love to spend two weeks on holiday in the sunshine in Barbados, but cannot afford to do so. My neighbour, however, is better off than I am and announces that he is shortly to take his family for the very two weeks in Barbados—something that I would really find so desirable. Off he goes. But how do I behave while he is away? I go around saying, 'Why would anyone want to go all the way to Barbados? It's far too hot there for one from our temperate climate. Besides, the novelty of those white sands, palm trees and blue seas must soon wear thin. All you get from a trip to Barbados is jetlag. I'm sticking to Bournemouth.' Sour grapes!

The expression 'sour grapes' originates from Old Testament times. It is used twice in the Old Testament in Jeremiah 31:29 and in Ezekiel 18:2. Jeremiah prophesied before and during Israel's exile to Babylon. Ezekiel prophesied in the exile in Babylon itself. Jeremiah's prophecy predates Ezekiel's by a short time. We thus quote from Jeremiah 31:29 as giving us the origin of the expression 'sour grapes': 'In those days they shall say no more: "The fathers have eaten sour grapes, and the children's teeth are set on edge"' (Jer. 31:29-30).

So what is God teaching here, through His servant Jeremiah? He is teaching individual responsibility and accountability—that we cannot 'pass the buck', but are responsible for ourselves, and one day will personally have to give an account before God. On that day we will be unable to blame others for our sins. Paul taught the same matter in the New Testament. In Romans 14:10 and the verses that follow he writes these words: 'But why do you judge your brother? Or why do you show contempt for your brother? For we shall all stand before the judgment seat of Christ... So then each of us shall give account of himself to God.'

A little later in the same chapter as the 'sour grapes' expression, Ezekiel further explained and amplified this notion of personal responsibility. We cannot blame others. 'The soul who sins shall die. The son shall not bear the guilt of the father, nor the father bear the guilt of the son. The righteousness of the righteous shall be upon himself, and the wickedness of the wicked shall be upon himself' (Ezek. 18:20).

Having to face God as our Judge on a coming day, with no one or nothing else to blame, understandably fills us with trepidation, for we know that we are sinners by nature and practice. Yet God's judgement is as certain as the day. 'For He is coming to judge the earth. With righteousness He shall judge the world, and the peoples with equity' (Ps. 98:9). And you can be sure too that God's judgement will be absolutely fair, for 'Shall not the Judge of all the earth do right?' (Gen. 18:25), and 'The LORD *is* righteous in all His ways' (Ps. 145:17)—including the final judgement.

The big question, therefore, is this: How do we prepare to face God when we will individually stand before His judgement bar? The answer of the Christian gospel is by faith in the Lord Jesus Christ. The gospel proclaims that because of Christ, and His death on the cross in the place of sinners, God Himself is righteous and that He is 'the justifier of [that is, He declares righteous] the one who has faith in Jesus' (Rom. 3:26).

The Gospel of Justification

The Bible certainly teaches the responsibility of individuals. Yet the Bible also teaches that if we belong to Jesus, He has taken the responsibility for us. He suffered the judgement that we should have received when He died for our sins at Calvary—He took the wrath of God which was our just due to avert that wrath from us. And also, the sinless life of Christ, given in sacrifice at Calvary, is actually credited to us when we put our faith in Jesus. We may thus be declared righteous by God, not because of our own merits—for we have none. Rather, we are declared righteous by God solely because of His grace to us in the Lord Jesus Christ. 'Justification' is the word which encapsulates all this. 'Justification' is the gospel preached by Paul and the gospel revealed in the New Testament. It truly is good news for condemned sinners who will, one day, have to stand before God on their own:

> Justification is an act of God's free grace wherein He pardoneth all our sins and accepteth us as righteous in His sight, only for the righteousness of Christ imputed to us and received by faith alone.[1]

Christians have a Saviour. Christ has taken responsibility for us. The bad news—and the gospel imperative—is that those outside of Christ will be responsible for their own sins on the Judgement Day, and so will be liable to God's wrath and a just retribution for all eternity. This will be more horrific than words can describe. Yet it won't be 'sour grapes', for the sinner will know that God is perfectly just and so will have no excuse or alibi. The central

---

1. Answer to Question 33 of the *Westminster Shorter Catechism*.

message of the Bible is that Christ died at Calvary to procure the salvation of sinners. He is the only Saviour. 'How shall we escape if we neglect so great a salvation ...?' (Heb. 2:3).

27

The blind leading the blind

'It's a case of the blind leading the blind.' When this expression is used, it is invariably found to be in a derogatory sense—perhaps of politicians, or those in charge in a work place. The expression is often one of exasperation. It suggests that those in authority are incompetent, out of touch with reality and don't really know what they are doing, and that their incompetence has negative repercussions on those they are leading.

It is debatable as to just how many people today realise that the expression about 'the blind leading the blind' actually originates from the lips of none less than the Lord Jesus Christ. He used it in denunciation of the religious leadership of His day—specifically of the Pharisees. He said of them: 'Let them alone. They are blind leaders of the blind. And if the blind leads the blind, both will fall into a ditch' (Matt. 15:14). The Saviour's description here is very vivid. It borders on being a cartoon painted in words. It is not difficult to believe that a smile was raised on the faces of His hearers when He uttered it.

Spiritual Blindness

To be physically blind is to be in a state of permanent darkness. According to the Bible, by nature we are all born in a state of spiritual darkness. We are blind to the reality of God and to our unfitness for fellowship with Him. We are blind to our need of the Lord Jesus to save us and we are blind to the consequent joy of salvation which flows from knowing Him. Salvation, however, occurs when, by the working of the Holy Spirit in our hearts, we are enlightened to all these matters and enabled to put our faith in the Jesus who once affirmed, 'I am the light of the world. He who follows Me shall not walk in darkness, but have the light of life' (John 8:12).

When the Lord Jesus ministered on earth, He gave sight to the physically blind. He is now enthroned in heaven, and from there He gives light to the spiritually blind. Salvation entails coming out of spiritual darkness into God's glorious light. 'For you were once darkness, but now *you are* light in the Lord' (Eph. 5:8). Salvation thus entails having our spiritual eyes opened—eyes once blinded by sin are now opened to the reality of Christ and His salvation:

> Amazing grace! How sweet the sound
> That saved a wretch like me!
> I once was lost but now am found;
> Was blind, but now I see.
>
> (John Newton, 1725–1807)

Follow the Leader?

When the Lord Jesus first uttered this expression concerning the blind leading the blind, He had in mind the Pharisees of His day. Luke records His saying on another occasion, 'And He spoke a parable to them: "Can the blind lead the blind? Will they not both fall into the ditch? A disciple is not above his teacher, but everyone who is perfectly trained will be like his teacher"' (Luke 6:39-40). Jesus was saying that if one is to lead others, he must first see the way clearly himself, otherwise disaster will result—the leader will lead others astray and into danger. If the leader falls into a pit, those following him will do so, too.

Jesus' condemnation of the Pharisees was stern. Why? Because 'For I bear them witness that they have a zeal for God, but not according to knowledge' (Rom. 10:2). Jesus condemned the religion proffered by the Pharisees as it was man-made and not God-given. He told of their 'teaching as doctrines the commandments of men' (Matt. 15:9). They were blinded by the age-old heresy that is still around—that salvation is by human merit rather than by divine mercy, by our own graft rather than by God's grace. In believing and practising this, and teaching that others should do the same, the Pharisees were 'the blind leading the blind'. They were spiritually dangerous, even perilous, as both they and those they taught would one day have to stand before God, and the insufficiency of their human efforts would be revealed. Eternal salvation can only be a divine blessing and gift. All else fails. Or, to change the metaphor, in the preceding verse Jesus said, 'Every plant which My heavenly Father has not planted will be uprooted' (Matt. 15:13).

The perils of 'the blind leading the blind' has important application for Christians today. We are told that 'we are what we eat.' Spiritually, we are a product of the pulpits under which we sit Sunday by Sunday. Those called to preach and teach the Word of God have a serious calling. How vital it is that those who have the spiritual oversight of us teach and preach what is 'of God' and not 'of man'. If they are in error, the whole congregation is in danger of being lead astray. If a false gospel is preached, detrimental, eternal consequences ensue. A preacher who is truly called of God will preach and teach the Word of God—nothing more, nothing less, nothing else. Paul stipulated that an elder or overseer is 'a steward of God' (that is, a manager of the revelation God has given) (Titus 1:7) and so hold 'fast the faithful word as he has been taught, that he may be able, by sound doctrine, both to exhort and convict those who contradict' (Titus 1:9). If a preacher is not true to God's Word, he will lead the gullible and untaught astray.

Our Protestant forefathers held tenaciously to the mottoes of 'The Bible alone', 'grace alone', 'faith alone' and 'Christ alone'. If we, too, hold to these and test all preaching and preachers by this touchstone, we will not be led astray. As a clear-sighted guide prevents his followers from falling into a pit and harming themselves, it is the truth of the gospel which delivers us from the fires of hell and ensures we will spend eternity in the nearer presence of the one true God—the God of eternal love, life and light.

28

The land of the living

Conflict concerning bedtime is not unknown in parent-children relationships! One childhood complaint that children have is that their parents send them to bed at night when they don't want to go to bed. Then, in the morning their parents make them get out of bed when they would rather stay in bed! When I was in school, my mother would sometimes knock on my bedroom door in the morning and say, 'Just checking that you are in the land of the living.'

The Ways of God
The expression 'the land of the living'—a shorthand for 'being alive'—is actually taken from the Bible. It is used there on more than one occasion and in more than one context. The Old Testament book of Job is commonly believed to be the oldest book in the world, set as it was some 2000 years B.C. The main character, Job, suffered dreadfully. In the permissive will of God, he lost his wealth, family and health almost overnight. Job was a godly man, and so, understandably, he was very perplexed at the Lord's dealings with him. How he longed to understand what was going on—but it all seemed so irrational! This led him to say, in exasperation, 'But where can wisdom be found? And where *is* the place of understanding? Man does not know its value, nor is it found *in the land of the living*' (Job 28:12,13).

We have to confess that none of us is omniscient as long as we live on earth in 'the land of the living'. 'For now we see in a mirror, dimly, but then face to face. Now I know in part, but then I shall know just as I also am known' (1 Cor. 13:12). In this fallen world, we are sure to experience divine providences—losses and crosses—which we can't fathom. Here, however, we are to exercise the faith and patience of Job, and leave our perplexities with God. We lack wisdom, yes, but 'God understands its way, and He knows its place' (Job 28:23). We won't always know the reason for what is going on in our lives—but God does. When we don't know, we know that He knows! So we may affirm with Job, 'But He knows the way that I take; *when* He has tested me, I shall come forth as gold' (Job 23:10). In the light of the Bible, we know that our God is too wise to make mistakes, and too loving to be unkind. He is God. He is perfectly entitled to move in a way which seems mysterious to us. He is not beholden to us—but He is infinitely worthy of our trust. A troubled saint once wrote:

> Judge not the Lord by feeble sense,
> But trust Him for His grace;
> Behind a frowning providence
> He hides a smiling face.

(William Cowper, 1731–1800)

The Christ of God

Isaiah 53 gives us one of the clearest views in the whole Bible of the atoning death of Christ at Calvary—even though it was written some 700 years before the actual event. Writing in the prophetic past tense, in the eighth verse of the prophecy, Isaiah foretold the following concerning Christ: 'He was taken from prison and from judgment, and who will declare His generation? For *He was cut off from the land of the living*; for the transgressions of My people He was stricken.'

Christ, in the fullness of time, was indeed 'cut off from the land of the living'. The death of Christ at Calvary takes us to the heart of the gospel. In the Bible, death, in its physical, spiritual and eternal facets, is revealed as a consequence of sin. It was imposed by God as a judgement for rebelling against Him. As we are all sinners, we are all liable to the punishment of death. The gospel, however, proclaims that Christ died in the place of sinners. He died to save us from divine judgement by taking that judgement on Himself, so that when we put our faith in Him we are delivered 'from the wrath to come' (1 Thess. 1:10) which is our due.

'Christ died for our sins' (1 Cor. 15:3).
'[He] Himself bore our sins in His own body on the tree' (1 Pet. 2:24).
'[He] was delivered up because of our offenses' (Rom. 4:25).

Respectfully, we may say that Christ achieved infinitely more by His dying than He did by His living, for salvation was wrought by His cross, not by His cradle. On the cross 'He was cut off from the land of the living; for the transgressions of My people He was stricken' (Isa. 53:8).

The Sufficiency of God

Before David was crowned king, he went through a very difficult time of being hunted and hounded by Saul. 1 Samuel 22 records that during this fraught time, he found shelter in a cave—the cave of Adullam. Moreover, Scripture makes it clear that during this time when his very life was threatened, David's ultimate refuge was not in a cave but in God Himself.

Psalm 142 is entitled 'A Contemplation of David. A Prayer when he was in the cave.' David's stress and distress is very evident from this Psalm: 'They have secretly set a snare for me... Refuge has failed me; No one cares for my soul' (vv. 3-4). But then David's faith broke through. He began to think not so much *logically* but *theologically*. In verse 5 we read, 'I cried out to You,

O LORD: I said, "You *are* my refuge, My portion in the land of the living."' And we know from the subsequent sacred history that David was eventually delivered from Saul, crowned king, and, through his line, the Messiah—the King of kings—was born. No natural or supernatural force can ever thwart the plans and purposes of God.

'You *are* ... My portion in the land of the living.' The God of the Bible is One who saves and sustains. David—in his tumultuous circumstances—knew the Lord as his all-sufficient 'portion'. So, too, may we. He has promised that His grace is sufficient for us (2 Cor. 12:9). If He doesn't give us a lighter load, He will surely strengthen our back to bear the load. If He doesn't change our circumstances, He will surely give us grace to cope with our circumstances. In difficult times we, too, may prove the adequacy and all-sufficiency of God—our 'portion in the land of the living'.

> He giveth more grace when the burdens grow greater,
> He sendeth more strength when the labors increase;
> To added affliction He addeth His mercy,
> To multiplied trials, His multiplied peace.
>
> When we have exhausted our store of endurance,
> When our strength has failed ere the day is half done,
> When we reach the end of our hoarded resources
> Our Father's full giving is only begun.
>
> His love has no limits, His grace has no measure,
> His power no boundary known unto men;
> For out of His infinite riches in Jesus
> He giveth, and giveth, and giveth again.
>
> (Annie Johnson Flint, 1866–1932)

29

There's a time and a place for everything

Is it true that 'there's a time and a place for everything'? The Christian's answer here is both yes and no. It's 'no' because there are certain things a Christian will not do, and certain places a Christian will not frequent. God's commandments contain prohibitions as well as positive enjoinments. If we aspire to live a life that is pleasing to God, we will be careful to obey both, as far as we are able.

Yet the above qualification notwithstanding, the expression 'There's a time and a place for everything' is very much a biblical one, for in Ecclesiastes 3:1, we read that 'to everything *there is* a season, a time for every purpose under heaven.' According to the Bible, everything which happens in time and space—in the world generally and in the lives of God's children particularly—is not accidental but providential. That is, absolutely everything that happens has been foreordained by the wisdom and love of God. Nothing happens 'by chance'. Everything is a result of God's eternal plan which He is currently bringing into effect by His omnipotent power. The goal of this plan is God's own glory, and the eternal blessing of His people. 'And we know that all things work together for good to those who love God, to those who are the called according to *His* purpose' (Rom. 8:28). As God is who He is—Almighty God—His plan and purpose will most surely be fulfilled. 'I know that You can do everything, and that no purpose *of Yours* can be withheld from You' (Job 42:2).

Our topic, therefore, is the providence of God. Questions 27 and 28 of the *Heidelberg Catechism* read as follow:

Q. What do you understand by the providence of God?
A. Providence is the almighty and ever-present power of God by which He upholds, as with His hand, heaven and earth and all creatures, and so rules them that leaf and blade, rain and drought, fruitful and lean years, food and drink, health and sickness, prosperity and poverty— all things, in fact, come to us not by change but from His fatherly hand.

Q. How does the knowledge of God's creation and providence help us?
A. We can be patient when things go against us, thankful when things go well, and for the future we can have good confidence in our faithful God and Father that nothing will separate us from His love. All creatures are so completely in His hand that without His will they can neither move nor be moved.

'There's a time and a place for everything.' Let us explore this a little further in the comforting light of God's providence.

Consider the Time of Your Birth
You did not ask to be born on such and such a date! Ultimately, this was the result of God's decree. God's words to Jeremiah the prophet also apply to us: 'Before I formed you in the womb I knew you' (Jer. 1:5).

Consider the Day of Your Death
This again will not be accidental but providential. In the eyes of the Almighty, there is no such thing as a premature death. He knew

the day of our death before the day of our birth, for He foreor-dained both. 'Your eyes saw my substance, being yet unformed. And in Your book they all were written, the days fashioned for me, when *as yet there were* none of them' (Ps. 139:16). We will not die before God's time, and we will not live for a moment after His time. A man is immortal until God's work is done.

Consider the Place of Your Residence

Where were you born, and where do you live and work? The answer is this: where God has placed you! 'He set the boundaries of the peoples' (Deut. 32:8). 'And He has made from one blood every nation of men to dwell on all the face of the earth, and has determined their preappointed times [how long we live] and the boundaries of their dwellings [where we live]' (Acts 17:26).

Consider the Pattern of Your Life

Our lives consist of a very colourful patchwork of people and events. We are born. We grow up. Perhaps we marry. We work. We retire. We die. We have good days. We have bad days. We have highs. We have lows. According to the Bible, all the details are embraced by God's providence. So it is that Ecclesiastes 7:13 and 14 guide us to 'consider the work of God; for who can make straight what He has made crooked? In the day of prosperity be joyful, but in the day of adversity consider: surely God has appointed the one as well as the other...'

Our Father in heaven knows what is best for His children. He sends us both sunshine and showers. He sends us both earthly and eternal blessings, for which we bow down before Him with humble thankfulness. He also sends us harsher providences—losses and crosses, and sorrows as well as joys. Here we bow down before Him in submission. He knows best. In these readings, I have often made the point that He is too wise to make mistakes and too loving to be unkind. Difficulties and devastations are actually blessings if they cast us on God more closely and cause us to seek His grace more fervently. Testing times are to be trusting times. It is in our inadequacy that we prove the total adequacy of our God. He promises us in these wonderful words that '[His] grace is sufficient for [us]' (2 Cor. 12:9).

Consider Your Salvation

Just as God predetermined the time and place of our birth, Scripture reveals that He decreed the time and place of our new birth as well. Salvation is the work of the Triune God and is His kindest providence of all in the lives of His children. Can you remember the time and place when and where you came to trust the Lord Jesus and enter into the joy of salvation? 1 Peter 1:2 teaches us that every believer is 'elect according to the foreknowledge of God the Father, in sanctification of the Spirit, for obedience and sprinkling of the blood of Jesus Christ'. According to the Bible, we are saved because before the foundation of the world God chose us to be saved. He sent His Son to procure our salvation at Calvary, and then, at His predetermined time in our lives, through the working of His Holy Spirit, He draws us to the crucified Saviour. He shows us both our need of Christ and the Christ for our need, and enables us to embrace Christ in His finished work and be eternally saved. Then, at the moment of our predetermined death, we enter into the nearer presence of our Saviour, and our salvation will be consummated. Death, for the believer, is the porter which ushers us into glory—'to depart and be with Christ, *which is* far better' (Phil. 1:23).

'There's a time and a place for everything.' This is certainly so from God's perspective. He has no problems. He only has plans which He will most certainly fulfil. 'For of Him and through Him and to Him *are* all things' (Rom. 11:36). It has been well said that those who can see the hand of God in everything can safely leave everything in the hand of God.

> My times are in Thy hand;
> My God, I wish them there;
> My life, my friends, my soul I leave
> Entirely to Thy care.
>
> My times are in Thy hand;
> Whatever they may be;
> Pleasing or painful, dark or bright,
> As best may seem to Thee.
>
> My times are in Thy hand;
> Why should I doubt or fear?
> My Father's hand will never cause
> His child a needless tear.
>
> My times are in Thy hand,
> I'll always trust in Thee;
> And, after death, at Thy right hand
> I shall forever be.

(William Freeman Lloyd, 1791–1853)

30
Touch wood

When talking to a colleague recently, I learnt that he was shortly due to retire. 'Touch wood,' he said. 'I'm in good health at the moment, and hopefully this will continue for a good few years.'

'Touch wood.' To 'touch wood' refers to a superstitious action which supposedly wards off undesirable things from happening to us. The superstition originated in pagan times. Certain trees were believed to be inhabited by evil spirits. Thus, if you made plans you would 'touch wood', with the belief that the evil spirits would be ignorant of your plans and so be unable to thwart them.

During the middle ages, the superstitious action of touching wood was 'Christianised'. It was the age of religious relics. Religious charlatans, out to make money from the gullible, used to sell pieces of wood which were purported to be from the actual cross of Christ. These were worn as a kind of 'lucky charm'. The gullible would touch the wood of the supposed cross, believing that this had power to ward off evil and bring them some kind of good fortune.

In Galatians 6:14 Paul exclaims, 'But God forbid that I should boast except in the cross of our Lord Jesus Christ, by whom the world has been crucified to me, and I to the world.' This reference to the true cross of Christ, which brings true eternal blessing, is not so much a reference to an inanimate object as it is to the atoning sacrifice which Christ made outside the walls of Jerusalem some 2,000 years ago. As the eternal Son of God, His sacrificial death on the cross has eternal validity. Salvation and eternal blessing were wrought, however, not by the *wood* of the cross but by the *work* of the cross—by the Christ who died there. Galatians 3:13 states that 'Christ has redeemed us from the curse of the law, having become a curse for us (for it is written, "Cursed *is* everyone who hangs on a tree").'

Superstition and superstitious actions are infinitely removed from the Christian faith, where the emphasis is not on what we do, but on what God in Christ at Calvary has done for us. The *sign* of the cross saves no one, but the *sacrifice* of the cross saves everyone who avails himself or herself of it by faith. The *emblem* of the cross is powerless to save, but the *expiation* of the cross is mighty to save. Christ is able to take our guilt away, for He was made accountable for our sins on the cross. A crucifix of wood or of metal is just a carefully constructed object. It cannot save. But the crucified Christ does save—as Christians on earth and in heaven can testify.

Our Means of Acceptance

The cross of Christ alone is the means through which we are accepted by God. In one of the most profound statements in the whole Bible, Paul writes in 2 Cor. 5:21, 'For He made Him who knew no sin *to be* sin for us, that we might become the righteousness of God in Him.' Paul here is explaining that on the cross of Calvary a great exchange and transaction occurred. On the cross the Sinless One bore the sins and punishment of others so that they might be spared that punishment. And because of the cross, guilty ones—all who put their faith in the crucified Saviour—are declared guiltless, that is, 'justified'.

Justification is an act of God's free grace wherein He pardoneth all our sins and accepteth us as righteous in

His sight, only for the righteousness of Christ imputed to us, and received by faith alone.[1]

Proof of God's Love

Secondly, the cross of Christ is the supreme expression of the love of God—who demonstrated 'at the present time His righteousness, that He might be just and the justifier of the one who has faith in Jesus' (Rom. 3:26). Almighty God is beholden to no one. He was well within His rights to condemn all sinners to eternal hell. But instead He had mercy, and sent His Son to die in the place of sinners and so rescue them from eternal hell. Romans 5:8 states that, 'God demonstrates His own love toward us, in that while we were still sinners, Christ died for us.' 1 John 4:10 reads: 'In this is love, not that we loved God, but that He loved us and sent His Son *to be* the propitiation for our sins.' We are to measure the love of God not by our fluctuating feelings or circumstances, but by the cross of Christ.

A Gospel to Proclaim

Thirdly, the cross of Christ is the gospel which Christians proclaim to a lost, perishing world. Good news is for sharing. The aim of evangelism is to get sinners to the foot of the cross. The Christian faith has its evangelistic imperative. The cross of Christ is God's roadblock to hell—and the only roadblock that there is. It has been well said that

> Between our sins and their reward,
> we set the passion of God's Son, our Lord.[2]

---

1. Answer to Question 33 of the *Westminster Shorter Catechism*.

2. These words are from the hymn 'And now, O Father, mindful of the love', W Bright, 1824-1901.

The Christian's Glory

Lastly, the cross of Christ alone is the Christian's true glory—and will be so for all eternity. The cross of Christ and the Christ of the cross have saved us from our sins and assured us of the right to a home in heaven. This being so, we concur with Paul and say, 'But God forbid that I should boast except in the cross of our Lord Jesus Christ ...' (Gal. 6:14). To know the crucified Saviour is to know the blessings and benefits He alone can bestow. Faith takes hold of the living Christ who saves—while superstition touches dead wood, which, as an inanimate object, is powerless to change anyone or anything.

> We sing the praise of Him who died,
> Of Him who died upon the cross;
> The sinners' hope let men deride,
> For this we count the world but loss.
>
> Inscribed upon that cross we see
> In shining letters 'God is Love.'
> He bears our sins upon the tree,
> He brings us mercy from above.
>
> The cross! it takes our guilt away.
> It holds the fainting spirit up,
> It cheers with hope the gloomy day,
> And sweetens every bitter cup.
>
> (Thomas Kelly, 1815)

31

Under a cloud

'I'm keeping a low profile, as I'm under a bit of a cloud.' We use the expression about being 'under a cloud' when we have made an embarrassing mistake, or, to use a different idiom, when we have 'dropped a clanger'. I remember once as a boy when I made myself some waffles. Foolishly, I didn't concentrate and they became very burnt. Almost before I could blink, the whole house was filled with blue smoke. The odour—to my chagrin—lingered for days and seemed to permeate every room. My dear mother, needless to say, was not too pleased. The incident put me 'under a cloud'.

In 1 Corinthians 10:1 Paul writes, 'Moreover, brethren, I do not want you to be unaware that all our fathers were *under the cloud*, all passed through the sea.' Paul was referring to the time of the Exodus from Egypt, the subsequent miracle at the Red Sea and the wilderness wandering of the people of Israel. In the Bible, however, the expression 'under the cloud' is used in the exact opposite way from which we commonly use it. To be 'under the cloud' in Bible times wasn't to be under disgrace, but in the sphere of blessing—to know the blessed presence, guidance and protection of Almighty God Himself, who is the fount of every blessing.

The building of the ancient tabernacle in Moses' time reached a climax in Exodus 40:34 when we read that, 'Then the cloud covered the tabernacle of meeting, and the glory of the LORD filled the tabernacle.' This cloud was what is known as a 'Theophany'—a visible appearance of the invisible God and a localised appearance of the One who is omnipresent. The cloud therefore refers to the actual presence of God with His people. The cloud was shown as guiding the Israelites—they followed the cloud.

> Whenever the cloud was taken up from above the tabernacle, the children of Israel would go onward in all their journeys. But if the cloud was not taken up, then they did not journey till the day that it was taken up (Exod. 40:36-37)

The cloud also protected the people. On the banks of the Red Sea, Israel was pursued by the armies of Pharaoh. They would have been overcome, had it not been for the cloud.

> And the Angel of God, who went before the camp of Israel, moved and went behind them; and the pillar of cloud went from before them and stood behind them. So it came between the camp of the Egyptians and the camp of Israel. Thus it was a cloud and darkness *to the one*, and it gave light by night *to the other*, so that the one did not come near the other all that night (Exod. 14:19-20).

Biblically speaking, therefore, who would not want to be 'under the cloud'? If God is with us, all can only be well. In Old Testament times, Almighty God 'In the daytime also ... led them with the cloud, and all the night with a light of fire' (Ps. 78:14). The cloud offered welcome protection from the fierce, Middle Eastern sun during the day, and the fire offered welcome warmth under the chilly, clear skies at night. But are there eternal principles to be gained from being 'under the cloud'? Yes, there are. From the cloud we learn the principles of both the divine presence and the divine guidance.

The Presence of God

The God of the Bible is One who graciously condescends to presence Himself with His people. He did so in the cloud, in Moses' day. He did so, supremely, in His Son, the Lord Jesus Christ. Jesus is the God-man—God in human flesh. Matthew 1:23 states that 'they shall call His name Immanuel," which is translated, "God with us."' As God in human form, Jesus is the unsurpassed and unsurpassable revelation of the one true God. Small wonder, then, that when Jesus raised a widow's son from death, the great crowd who were there at the funeral procession exclaimed out loud, 'God has visited His people' (Luke 7:16).

Today, every believer is privileged to know the personal presence of God in the Person of His Holy Spirit. 'Or do you not know that your body is the temple of the Holy Spirit *who is* in you, whom you have from God, and you are not your own?' (1 Cor. 6:19). The indwelling of the Holy Spirit is every Christian's new-birth right. The Holy Spirit is the presence of God with us day by day, through all the ups and downs of life. Thank God for His Holy Spirit. His indwelling enables us to say, 'Yea, though I walk through the valley of the shadow of death, I will fear no evil; for You *are* with me' (Ps. 23:4). According to the Bible, safety is not the absence of evil but the presence of God.

The Guidance of God

'In the daytime also He led them with the cloud' (Ps. 78:14). And the God of the Bible still guides His children. How? He does so by His Word and by His providence.

The Word of God

'Your word *is* a lamp to my feet and a light to my path' (Ps. 119:105). If we desire to know the will of God, we have to read the Word of God. He guides us by His Word. 'For best results, follow the Maker's instructions.' The Bible is our Maker's manual. It is indispensable for a happy life, a happy death and a happy eternity.

The Providence of God

'God's works of providence are His most holy, wise and powerful preserving and governing all His creatures and all their actions.'[1] God guides us day by day. He is in charge of the universe in general and of His children's lives in particular. His will unfolds a day at a time. Mercifully, He does not reveal all at once what is ahead of us. We are thus to trust Him one day at a time, for the next step. God knows best. He opens some doors and closes others. He gives us abilities to use and develop. He leads certain people across our paths. He puts us in certain settings and situations. 'He leads me in the paths of righteousness for His name's sake' (Ps. 23:3). He sends blessings. He sends us difficulties to cast us on Him and His grace more closely, and to eradicate any sense of self-sufficiency on our part. His wisdom knows how to balance or blend both the sunshine and storms which come to us. Whatever happens, He never fails His children. 'The steps of a *good* man are ordered by the LORD, and He delights in his way. Though he fall, he shall not be utterly cast down; for the LORD upholds *him with* His hand' (Ps. 37:23-24).

'Under a cloud.' The popular view is that this is a negative term with negative connotations. But if we know our Bibles, we would rather be nowhere else! In the Bible this term refers to the presence, guidance and protection of God which will be the blessed portion of His children until they safely reach their eternal home.

---

1. Answer to Question 11 of the *Westminster Shorter Catechism.*

Under a cloud

Open now the crystal fountain,
Whence the healing stream doth flow;
Let the fire and cloudy pillar
Lead me all my journey through.
Strong Deliv'rer …
Be Thou still my Strength and Shield …

(William Williams, 1717–91)

32

What a godsend!

A 'godsend' refers to someone or something which arrives unexpectedly, and at just the right time to meet a need or emergency. An elderly lady collapses in the street—but a doctor happens to be passing at the same time; your car breaks down in the middle of heavy traffic—but thankfully, you are a member of the RAC or AA, whom you are able to contact. They arrive and get you up and running again; you have lost your way in a strange town—but a local person notices your puzzled look and body language, and points you where you wish to go; you've had a horrendously bad day at the office—and the pastor calls on you in the evening. You can share your burdens with him and then take them to the Lord in prayer. When such happens the expression might be uttered: 'What a godsend!'

The exact expression—'a godsend'—is not found in the Bible. Yet the idea is most definitely there. The God of the Bible is revealed as a God who sends. Out of His abounding mercy, He sends to alleviate His children's need.

The Bread Sent from Heaven

In early Old Testament times, God's people found themselves in slavery in Egypt. But under God, Moses delivered them from their cruel bondage. 'This Moses ... God sent *to be* a ruler and a deliverer by the hand of the Angel who appeared to him in the bush' (Acts 7:35). Having escaped from the cruelty of their Egyptian taskmasters, the people of Israel wandered in the wilderness for forty years. The wilderness is a barren place—a desert. In the wilderness, all that is not of God will die. So how did the Israelites survive? Only by the goodness of God. 'He ... satisfied them with the bread of heaven. He opened the rock, and water gushed out; it ran in the dry places *like* a river' (Ps. 105:40-41).

The 'bread' in question here was the manna that God provided. This truly was a 'godsend'. It was a miraculous provision, every day—except each Sabbath—for forty years. The day before the Sabbath, God ensured that a double portion of manna was given. This, when kept for the Sabbath, was not subject to the process of decay. When the Israelites entered the Promised Land after their forty years of wandering, however, the Bible informs us that 'the children of Israel no longer had manna, but they ate the food of the land of Canaan that year' (Josh. 5:12). In the wilderness, God sent manna—a miraculous provision, for nothing grows in the desert. God's provision was supernatural. Yet when the Israelites entered Canaan, they had no need of a miraculous provision. Daily bread now was obtained by cultivating the land. God's provision now was through natural means, rather than through supernatural means—and in this the children of Israel were able to acknowledge their dependence on Him for a good harvest.

The one, overriding lesson of the manna is that God undertakes for His people. He provides for our needs—though He does not indulge our greeds. Philippians 4:19 assures us that '... God shall supply all your need according to His riches in glory by Christ Jesus.'

The Saviour Sent from Heaven
'What a godsend!' The ultimate, unsurpassed and unsurpassable Godsend of all takes us to the very core of the Bible's message. We refer to God's sending of His own Son into the world to save

sinners. Our deepest need is for a Saviour. Christ is God's own provision for our deepest need. 'But when the fullness of the time had come, God sent forth His Son, born of a woman, born under the law, to redeem those who were under the law, that we might receive the adoption as sons' (Gal. 4:4-5). 'In this is love, not that we loved God, but that He loved us and sent His Son *to be* the propitiation for our sins' (1 John 4:10). 'For God did not send His Son into the world to condemn the world, but that the world through Him might be saved' (John 3:17).

Jesus, therefore, is the ultimate Godsend. We are condemned sinners, but Jesus is the Saviour of sinners. We are under the wrath of God, but Jesus delivers us from the wrath of God. We are alienated from God, but Jesus reconciles us to God. We are 'sinners in the hands of an angry God' (to use a phrase from Jonathan Edwards), but through the precious blood shed for us at Calvary, our sins are forgiven and forgotten by God the Father. A 'godsend' is a true godsend when it meets a need. Christ alone is the Saviour and His salvation meets our deepest need. He is God's gracious provision for condemned sinners. Where would we be without this incomparable Godsend?

33

You've kept the best until last

In 2003 England won the Rugby World Cup. The victory was achieved on the very last kick of the game—specifically by a drop goal kicked expertly by Jonny Wilkinson, the Number 10. Great rejoicing ensued. It was commonly agreed that the best was kept until last.

'Keeping the best until last' is a practice used by some as a ploy. At Christmas-time, parents often keep the main present for their children until the time after they have opened lesser presents. The suspense heightens the appreciation. A firework display usually ends on a spectacular cascade—a humdinger—and a pop concert usually concludes with a rousing, rowdy hit. The idea is to send the visitors away happy. Thus the best is kept until last.

While we won't find the exact words 'You've kept the best until last' in the Bible, in John 2:10 we find a near equivalent. In John 2:10 these words are written: 'Every man at the beginning sets out the good wine, and when the *guests* have well drunk, then the inferior. You have kept the good wine until now!' The words were spoken by a steward at a wedding feast in Cana in Galilee—a feast to which the Lord Jesus was invited. The occasion was a significant one, as it was there that the Lord Jesus performed His first miracle while here on earth—the miracle of turning water into wine.

So picture a wedding at Cana in Galilee. Jesus, Mary—His earthly mother—and His disciples had all been invited. Wedding feasts in Bible times went on for many days. To the great embarrassment of the groom, however, after a few days the wine ran out. His hospitality had appeared to fail. Mary informed Jesus, and Jesus told the servants at the feast to fill with water the six thirty-gallon jars that were there for Jewish, ceremonial washing. This they did. Having done so, He commanded the servants to draw some of the water out and take it to the steward of the feast to taste. This they also did, and after the task was complete, amazingly, it was found that the plain water had been transformed into the most wonderful wine. The servants were 'in' on the miracle. The steward, however, wasn't. He knew good wine, though! He also knew that it was not out of order to serve lesser quality wine later on in a feast, for by that time, alcohol had somewhat dulled the discernment of the guests. The steward was thus puzzled to find such high-quality wine at this stage in the wedding celebration. And so he remarked, 'Every man at the beginning sets out the good wine, and when the *guests* have well drunk, then the inferior. You have kept the good wine until now!'

Jesus Christ is God

But what do we learn from Jesus' first miracle of turning water into wine—when the best was kept until last? First of all, the miracle reveals the deity of the Lord Jesus. A mere man could not instantly turn water into wine. Only God the great Creator could perform such a feat. John actually terms Jesus' miracles as 'signs'. A 'sign' is a pointer. This sign points out the identity of Jesus—He is the Son of God and God the Son. The sign confirmed Jesus' disciples' faith in Him. John concludes the remarkable incident by saying, 'This beginning of signs Jesus did in Cana of Galilee, and manifested His glory; and His disciples believed in Him' (John 2:11). Glory is, uniquely, an attribute of

God. Thus Jesus alone could say 'He who has seen Me has seen the Father' (John 14:9).

Jesus Changes Lives

Secondly, the miracle at Cana reveals the transforming power of the Lord Jesus. What a difference He makes! There is a vast difference between plain water and splendid wine—and there is an infinite difference between a Christian and a non-Christian. The Bible says 'Therefore, if anyone *is* in Christ, *he is* a new creation; old things have passed away; behold, all things have become new' (2 Cor. 5:17). Jesus changes lives and destinies. Knowing Him is the difference between salvation and condemnation, being a child of wrath or a child of God, and spending eternity in heaven rather than in hell.

Interestingly, in Old Testament times, Moses also, under God, performed a transforming miracle involving water. In Egypt, he 'he lifted up the rod and struck the waters that *were* in the river, in the sight of Pharaoh and in the sight of his servants. And all the waters that *were* in the river were turned to blood' (Exod. 7:20). John 1:17 reminds us that the law was given through Moses. The law of Moses reveals our sin. We have broken God's law and are thus condemned sinners in His sight, liable to pay the penalty for breaking it. Yet John 1:17 in full states: 'For the law was given through Moses, *but* grace and truth came through Jesus Christ.' Jesus came to redeem us from the penalty of breaking God's law. He died on the cross to procure our forgiveness. He died on the cross to reconcile us to God. He died on the cross to bring us into God's family for time and for eternity. The law of Moses condemns us—water into blood. Jesus saves us. He gives us new and eternal life—water into wine.

In the Bible, wine is a symbol of cheer. Psalm 104:15 tells of 'wine *that* makes glad the heart of man'. None can cheer the heart like Jesus. True joy is knowing Him and His salvation. In the abundance of wine which He provided at Cana in Galilee we gain a glimpse of the abundance of life He came to bring sinners. Jesus said, 'I have come that they may have life, and that they may have *it* more abundantly' (John 10:10). And at the end of our earthly life, when we meet Him face to face and are ushered into God's eternal home of light and joy, will we not also be impelled to confess to Him, 'Lord, you have kept the best until now'?

SOLI DEO GLORIA

Also available from

Christian Focus Publications

TIMOTHY CROSS

A LITTLE BIRD TOLD ME

Everyday Expressions
from Scripture

ISBN 978-1-78191-553-0

A LITTLE BIRD TOLD ME

Everyday Expressions from Scripture

TIMOTHY CROSS

'The writing is on the wall', 'a drop in the ocean' and 'from strength to strength'. Just some of our everyday expressions which find their roots in the Bible! People quote biblical expressions without even knowing that they are doing so. Historically, the influence of the Bible has been so great that it has permeated the very fibre of the English language. Timothy Cross in this enlightening and Scripture rooted book reveals the origins of these sayings and considers their meaning.

Christian Focus Publications

Our mission statement –

STAYING FAITHFUL
In dependence upon God we seek to impact the world through
literature faithful to His infallible Word, the Bible. Our aim is to
ensure that the Lord Jesus Christ is presented as the only hope
to obtain forgiveness of sin, live a useful life and look forward to
heaven with Him.

Our books are published in four imprints:

CHRISTIAN
FOCUS

Popular works including biographies,
commentaries, basic doctrine and
Christian living.

CHRISTIAN
HERITAGE

Books representing some of the best
material from the rich heritage of
the church.

MENTOR

Books written at a level suitable for
Bible College and seminary students,
pastors, and other serious readers.
The imprint includes commentaries,
doctrinal studies, examination of current issues and church history.

CF4•K

Children's books for quality Bible
teaching and for all age groups: Sunday
school curriculum, puzzle and activity
books; personal and family devotional
titles, biographies and inspirational
stories – because you are never too
young to know Jesus!

Christian Focus Publications Ltd,
Geanies House, Fearn, Ross-shire,
IV20 1TW, Scotland, United Kingdom.
www.christianfocus.com
blog.christianfocus.com